THEY USED GUERRILLA WEAPONS . . . AND EARNED MORE CASH

- A business that conducts most of its transactions in the morning was able to better its investment in advertising and direct mail by investing in—ready? Fresh coffee and doughnuts.

- A very successful employment agency actually wallpapers one wall of each reception area with testimonial letters, enabling success to beget success.

- A furniture store used only a single billboard upon which it could legitimately say "next exit" and grew to enormity starting with that weapon.

- A chain, which received all its initial leads by telephone, improved its lead conversion rate 22% simply by teaching telephone demeanor.

- A fund-raising organization dramatically improved its speed of collections by rewording its invoice and treating it as a marketing weapon.

YOU CAN TOO!

JAY CONRAD LEVINSON is a former vice-president and creative director at J. Walter Thompson Advertising and Leo Burnett Advertising. He now runs his own marketing consultancy, and his clients include both Fortune 500 companies and start-up organizations. He lectures nationally and is the author of *Guerrilla Marketing, Guerrilla Marketing Attack,* and *The Ninety-Minute Hour.*

Other Books by Jay Conrad Levinson:

THE MOST IMPORTANT $1.00 BOOK EVER WRITTEN

SECRETS OF SUCCESSFUL FREE-LANCING

SAN FRANCISCO: AN UNUSUAL GUIDE TO UNUSUAL SHOPPING (with John Bear and Pat Levinson)

EARNING MONEY WITHOUT A JOB

555 WAYS TO EARN EXTRA MONEY

GUERRILLA MARKETING

AN EARTHLING'S GUIDE TO SATELLITE TV

150 SECRETS OF SUCCESSFUL WEIGHT LOSS

SMALL BUSINESS SAVVY
(with K. Barton Henrie)

QUIT YOUR JOB!

GUERRILLA MARKETING ATTACK

THE NINETY-MINUTE HOUR

GUERRILLA MARKETING WEAPONS

100 AFFORDABLE MARKETING METHODS FOR MAXIMIZING PROFITS FROM YOUR SMALL BUSINESS

JAY CONRAD LEVINSON

A PLUME BOOK

PLUME
Published by the Penguin Group
Penguin Books USA Inc., 357 Hudson Street,
New York, New York 10014, U.S.A.
Penguin Books Ltd. 27 Wrights Lane,
London W8 5TZ, England
Penguin Books Australia Ltd. Ringwood,
Victoria, Australia
Penguin Books Canada Ltd. 10 Alcorn Avenue,
Toronto, Ontario, Canada M4V 3B2
Penguin Books (N.Z.) Ltd. 182-190 Wairau Road
Auckland 10, New Zealand

Penguin Books Ltd. Registered Offices:
Harmondsworth, Middlesex, England

First Published by Plume, an Imprint of Dutton Signet, a division of Penguin
Books USA Inc.

First Printing, November, 1990
15

 REGISTERED TRADEMARK—MARCA REGISTRADA

Library of Congress Cataloging-in-Publication Data

Levinson, Jay Conrad.
   Guerrilla marketing weapons : 100 affordable marketing methods for maximizing
profits from your small business / by Jay Conrad Levinson.
      p.   cm.
   ISBN 0-452-26519-3
   1. Marketing.   2. Small business—Management.   3. Advertising.
I. Title
HF5415.L479   1990
658.8—dc20   90-7329
                                                                            CIP

PRINTED IN THE UNITED STATES OF AMERICA
Set in Times Roman
Designed by Leonard Telesca

Dedicated with gratitude
to Bill Shear, John Maxwell, Mike Larsen, and Elizabeth Pomada for escorting this book from my head to your hands; to Seth Meyer Robert Pickett for being my first grandson; to Amy Malka Levinson and Bill Pickett for having Seth; and especially to Patsy Levinson for having Amy and putting up with me.

It is not easy to live with a guerrilla.

CONTENTS

PREFACE

Is there truly a need for three books on guerrilla marketing? After all, I've already written *Guerrilla Marketing* and *Guerrilla Marketing Attack*. Does the business world honestly require *Guerrilla Marketing Weapons*?

You bet it does. The business community honestly requires this book and about five hundred more books on marketing for the small and medium-size businesses of the 1990s—especially those high on ambition but low on funds.

Marketing is growing in size and intricacy while it's changing every month. No one book on marketing can ever do more than capture a glimmer of the wisdom about the topic.

In *Guerrilla Marketing Attack*, I touched on all 100 of the weapons investigated in this book. Because of the limitations of space, I could allot only three or four lines to each weapon. In this book, I can devote two pages to each. In *Guerrilla Marketing*, I looked into only 18 of the guerrilla marketing weapons; I did not examine the other 82. Why? Because marketing is becoming more comprehensive and I am becoming less ignorant.

Learn about these guerrilla marketing weapons. Use as many as are appropriate to your goals. The weapons, and therefore the profits, of guerrillas are bountiful.

1

THE MORE WEAPONS YOU USE, THE MORE PROFITS YOU EARN

Conventional weapons are utilized to inflict harm. Guerrilla marketing weapons are utilized to generate profits. If any harm's to be done, it will be to your competition. The damage won't be to their bodies, only to their bottom lines.

In fact, a weapon may be defined, according to any self-respecting guerrilla, as a method of communication or contact with customers and prospects designed to render service, improve quality, clarify benefits, enhance credibility, or make the customer or prospect feel good.

Guerrilla marketing weapons don't have much in common with conventional weapons, as you can easily surmise. But they do have five important similarities:

1. Guerrilla marketing weapons are designed to be used by pros, not by amateurs. These weapons are not for playing games. Their use requires skill.
2. Guerrilla marketing weapons work best when combined with other weaponry; the larger your arsenal, the wider your grin when you review your cash flow.

3. Guerrilla marketing weapons may appear innocent, but they can be frighteningly dangerous when misused —as they frequently are.
4. Guerrilla marketing weapons can help you achieve glittering victories, sending your opposition down to bitter defeat. This book has been written to help you do just that.
5. Guerrilla marketing weapons themselves don't win or lose marketing wars; people do. What you do with your weapons makes the critical difference.

Let me be candid with you before you go on. This book covers 100 guerrilla marketing weapons. Is that all there are? Of course not. There may be 200 weapons, even 1,000 in time. I have purposely limited my list to 100, but this is no reason for you to limit yours. After you've evaluated the weapons in this book, I hope you'll invent your own new weapons; stay alert to the development of other new weapons, and always be ready to add to your arsenal. Reread the title of this chapter to see why.

What you hold in your hands is both the key to the arsenal and an invaluable sourcebook. Unlike conventional weaponry, many of the guerrilla marketing weapons are absolutely free. If you're a student of guerrilla marketing— and you'd better be to survive in the fiercely competitive environment of the 1990s and beyond—you know full well that guerrilla marketing requires that you invest time, energy, and imagination in your marketing, not simply huge amounts of dollars. This book gives you ample opportunity to make those investments.

To be sure your efforts pay off handsomely, I sincerely recommend that you read *Guerrilla Marketing* and *Guerrilla Marketing Attack*. After all, to be a guerrilla with your weaponry, you should first be a guerrilla with your head, heart, soul, and spirit.

Feel good deep inside that the vast majority of your competitors are not aware of 100 marketing weapons. Perhaps they know only 15 weapons, or possibly as few as 5. I'll bet most of your competitors are actually using only 1, 2, or 3 weapons.

Child's play! You will be aware of all 100 weapons. You will utilize 40, 50, or possibly even more. My average client uses 47.

Once, I was giving a lecture on guerrilla marketing to an audience of about two hundred business owners. I spent an hour rattling off my full list of 100 weapons. Then, I asked for audience participation.

"How many of you," I asked, "are using between zero and ten weapons? Answer by raising your hands." A handful of hands shot up. "How many are using between ten and twenty?" More hands were raised. "Between twenty and thirty?" Fewer hands. "Between thirty and forty?" Hardly any hands. "Between forty and fifty?" One or two hands.

Finally, I asked, "Anyone using more than fifty weapons?" A man in the middle of the room raised his hand sheepishly. "You're using more than fifty guerrilla marketing weapons?" I inquired.

"I'm using eighty-four," responded the man with his hand raised to the ceiling. "That's wonderful!" I said. "It's not so wonderful," he said. "I'm ignoring sixteen weapons."

Turns out that the man with the 84 weapons was president of a leading chain of weight-loss clinics with over three hundred offices throughout America. It also turns out that he later hired me to help him activate some of the other 16 weapons he wasn't using. I guess some people are natural-born guerrillas. This guy certainly was. And his bank account proved it.

If you don't have innate guerrilla tendencies, though I suspect you may have them simply because you're reading this book, rest assured that guerrilla marketing tactics can be learned. They need not be part of your DNA.

Look at the list of weapons in the Contents and consider how many you are using right now. Then, realize that you are offered information about a host of new weapons. The addition of even 1 or 2 new weapons to your own arsenal can make a dramatic difference to your financial statement.

Think of the effect of an additional 11 or 12 . . . or 42!

When you've completed this book, if you don't add a whole slew of new weapons to your arsenal, one of us is nuts. I was paid well to write this book, and I had a whale of a time doing it. So you're the guilty party if you don't use this information to add potency to your marketing attack and plentitude to your profits.

Understand that these weapons are strictly oriented to your *profits*. Some misguided souls, obviously not guerrillas, use these weapons to bolster their sales, their volume, their turnover, their egos. Don't fall into those traps!

Guerrilla marketing weapons should be employed to increase your profits. The other goals are foolish. Anyone can boost sales with sufficient marketing. But they can lose money in the process. Very unguerrillalike. Anyone can enlarge volume and turnover with these weapons. But that is not the intent of these pages.

Many people pamper their egos with these weapons. They are smitten with the idea of seeing their businesses in the newspaper, their names on television, their offers in the mail. Take my word, these are not guerrillas. These are game-players, and some may be simpletons. Guerrillas see to it that their investments of time, energy, imagination, and money pay off in pure, delicious profits. If ego gratification is a by-product, well, that's just fine. But that's the side dish, not the main course.

If you're like most businesspeople on planet Earth, you probably think that marketing weapons cost money. Guess what? You're only half right.

Of the 100 guerrilla marketing weapons, 50 do cost money, to be sure. In some cases, it is merely a pittance, such as the cost to produce reprints of publicity stories or run off a batch of circulars.

But fully half of these weapons are completely free! In

this book they are boxed for easy reference. They do require the investment of time, energy, and imagination, but they ask for zero investment of money. I wonder how many of these free weapons you are using at this moment. I wonder how many you'll use when you complete this book.

When I told you that my average client uses 47 of these weapons, I neglected to mention that in many cases the client isn't paying a cent for 37 of them. Yet it's true.

In many cases, the free weapon will be more effective than the paid weapon. Radio talk show interviews almost always outpull radio commercials. Naturally. That's a function of a sixty-minute commercial over a sixty-second commercial. Still, both are radio. And one weapon is free.

100 Guerrilla Marketing Weapons, Neatly Categorized

How should I present these weapons to you? In alphabetical order? By rank of importance? In order of popularity? No. None of those categories does these weapons justice. The categories must jiggle your brain a bit so you can see how many weapons fit together.

There are proper times and places for all guerrilla marketing weapons. Let's start with the first of eight categories to prove that point:

1. *Weapons for the outset.* Fourteen weapons fall into this category. Even if your outset is past and gone, it's a smart idea to review these weapons and determine how well you're using them.
2. *Weapons not recognized as part of marketing.* If you don't have these 16 weapons in your current arsenal, you'll have some of them soon. When you do, it's necessary that you understand these are part of marketing.
3. *Weapons that begin with attitudes.* Many of these dozen weapons are the secret to the success of a surprisingly

high number of companies. Just because many are free doesn't mean they're easy to use with skill.

4. *Weapons overlooked by nonguerrillas.* Several of these 18 weapons can justifiably lay claim to the greatest effectiveness of any weapon. It's tough to argue with guerrillas who have used them to earn fortunes.

5. *Weapons that make you easy to buy from.* Although a few of these 9 weapons might fit into other categories, the category chosen makes the most sense. If you're not easy to buy from in the 1990s, you're a goner.

6. *Weapons that are frequently misused.* These 8 weapons fit several categories, but none as important as this one. Guerrillas don't just use weapons; they employ them with expertise and effectiveness.

7. *Weapons that produce instant results.* Wait! Don't go scurrying over to this category (Chapter 8, if you must) to activate its 16 weapons until you've considered the other guerrilla marketing weapons.

8. *Weapons that have extra firepower.* It's well and good to use marketing weapons that cost not one penny, but it's even more fulfilling to use 7 weapons that can blast your competitors to smithereens.

If you're a right-thinking guerrilla, you'll recognize the need to look into every one of these categories. Even if you're in an established firm, you'll want to check that you didn't miss anything at the outset. You'll want to see which weapons aren't known to be part of marketing but definitely are. You'll probably want to run an attitude check on yourself and your people. You won't want to overlook any potential profit producer. Of course you'll want to make it easy to buy what you sell. You'll wonder if you're misusing any of the weapons right now. You'll be fascinated by the concept of instant results in marketing. And as a guerrilla, you'll want to learn about marketing weapons that produce maxiprofits from mass markets.

You read it here first: The key to successfully marketing

a business is not looking into all these eight categories, but all 100 of these weapons. You never know when a weapon can be a prime reason for your victory:

- A furniture store used only a single billboard, on which they could legitimately say only NEXT EXIT, and grew to hugeness starting with that weapon.
- A national chain, which received all its initial leads by telephone, improved its lead conversion rate by 22 percent simply by teaching telephone demeanor.
- A large fund-raising organization dramatically improved its speed of collections by rewording its invoice and treating it as a marketing weapon.
- A giant printing and copying firm got that way by running giant yellow pages ads in every available color, appearing ultracredible to the many prospects who use the yellow pages to select a printing or copying firm.
- A very successful employment agency actually wall-papers one wall of each reception area with testimonial letters, enabling success to beget success.
- A business that conducts most of its transactions in the morning was able to better its investment in advertising and direct mail by investing in—ready?—fresh coffee and doughnuts.
- An urgent-care center solidified its repeat and referral business by handsomely framing an article written by the physician in charge and hanging it in the reception lobby.

Most of these businesses didn't learn about these marketing methods in textbooks. You can be sure they examined many weapons, testing them, evaluating them, then investing further or discarding them, and ending up with precision firepower in their marketing.

To gain that power, the kind that comes with a broad array of potent weapons, keep an open mind when considering every single weapon. You're not too big for any of them. The largest corporation in America boosted its profits by millions by virtue of a single personal letter to a key member of another corporation. In these days of direct mail, personal letters, with warm personal comments, have come to be overlooked. But not by guerrillas.

As you look into these weapons, keep clearly in mind that the simplest of your tasks will be to select which you want to use. That requires only reading and thinking.

Your weapons will work to the maximum and earn the maximum income for you if you properly take them through four steps:

1. *Selection:* This is easy as pie because you can do it merely by reading this book and making notes on a handy pad. Select a lot of weapons. Earn a lot of money. There's a direct correlation.

2. *Prioritization:* You might be overwhelmed when you first look at this list of weapons you've decided to activate. Nobody said you had to launch them all at once. First, put them into priority order—which you'll do first, second, third, and so on down the line.

3. *Inauguration:* This is where the wimps get weeded from the guerrillas. Launching your guerrilla marketing weapons is the toughest part, takes the most time, costs the most money (but far less than conventional marketing), and puts your energy where your dreams are.

4. *Maintenance:* This is easier than inauguration, but harder than selection or prioritization. A majority of the weapons require maintenance in order to work in the first place, so you'll have to address yourself to the care and feeding of your marketing.

The selection of your weapons should be accomplished with an eye toward only those you can use properly. It might be nice to employ 60 weapons, but if you're going to botch up 40 of them, you'll be better off starting with a list of 20. Although I urge you to utilize as many weapons as possible, that urgency is tempered with a note of caution. Select weapons that can be professionally produced, well maintained, and devoid of any hint of amateurism.

Your selection should be made with a combination of experimentation and commitment. Although you want to test to see which weapons best help you accomplish your goals, many of the weapons require commitment in order for them to succeed. One or two newspaper ads aren't going to prove or disprove the efficacy of newspaper for you. Here, a three-month commitment of at least one ad per week must be made. But you might prove the power of a free seminar with just one shot at it.

Prioritizing your weapons requires a sense of reality. Be careful you don't bring in more leads or traffic than you can handle. Don't launch too many weapons at once. Be sure there's someone to oversee the proper launching and maintenance of the weapon. The weapon that appears most attractive to you might be the sixth you'll launch, rather than the first, for any of a number of reasons.

Inaugurating the weapons is the step that requires the most pure action. Now you leave the ivory tower and hunker down in the trenches. That time, energy, and imagination I talked about? Here's where you'll need it—all of it.

Everything you do has got to be right: determining your target audience, making sure every word and picture conveys the right ideas to the right people in the right media, making the right offer at the right time. Selecting and prioritizing your weapons were risk-free activities. Inaugurating them puts a lot on the line—your time and your money, to mention but two examples.

When you are launching your marketing weapons, you are keeping promises you have made to yourself. These promises come in the form of your marketing strategy and your decisions about weapon utilization. It's easy to make promises. It's tough to keep them. But guerrillas keep the promises they make—to themselves, to their customers, and to their employees. Your mettle as a guerrilla will be proven as you activate your weapons.

Up till this point, you've surveyed the beach, studied the waves, and become aware of the tides and currents. Now it's time to dive in. You'll get wet, but your prioritization will prevent you from getting in over your head—or drowning.

Don't expect miracles. You'll work smart and hard to launch your weapons. When you do, you'll be establishing the momentum that can lead to your success. Realize that and you'll have more contentment and fewer ulcers than if you expect a sudden windfall of profits.

As you gain confidence in yourself as a marketing guerrilla, your public will gain confidence in your company.

After about a year, you'll be able to remove some weapons from your arsenal because they're less cost-effective than others. You'll also notice that several weapons are superstars, so you'll most likely want to reprioritize your list. You may want to inaugurate a few new weapons. And your maintenance will become simpler because you'll begin to discover the timesaving and profit-producing benefits of delegation. Many guerrilla marketing tasks are delegatable.

Eventually, you'll be in the enviable situation of utilizing the same weapons over and over, concentrating on using them better and better.

The other day, I asked a client why he canceled his advertising schedule in a major national newspaper. I knew that for every $100 he put into the newspaper, he earned $1,000 in profits. "The other fourteen papers are pulling better," he said.

If you aren't going to find the process of guerrilla marketing to be exciting, enticing, and enjoyable, I strongly urge you to assign the task to someone else inside or outside of your organization: your designated guerrilla.

Marketing the high quality and service you offer while reaping handsome rewards from your efforts is one of the business world's most valuable gifts to the business practitioner. Far too many misguided entrepreneurs in this world offer gold-medal quality and service, yet struggle to pay their bills, let alone stay in business.

Their only missing component is marketing. Once that marketing plugs them into their target audience, and their benefits emerge from under the bushel, their companies prosper.

Old-fashioned thinking prohibited the small business from marketing aggressively because of a shortage of cash. But guerrilla thinking encourages the small business to market aggressively even without cash. If you have a shortage of cash, time, energy, and imagination, and are unable to delegate your marketing to others who, while not requiring cash, do have the other virtues, you're just not going to be a guerrilla.

But I have this deep-seated feeling that once you realize how many marketing weapons you can use, and see the impact these can have upon your profitability, you'll find either the time, energy, and imagination or the people who can supply them for you.

I hope you have the guts to get egg on your face. I hope you dare to experiment with these weapons. You might make a mistake or two, but you might strike gold in a hidden vein. If you're not making any mistakes, you're either brilliant or too conservative. Only you will know which.

The reason I grant you the freedom to screw up is so that you'll be relatively uninhibited about the marketing process. Only if you try many weapons will you know which will be the most devastating in your arsenal. It should be a well-stocked arsenal. But it won't be if you don't take chances.

Once, along with several fellow executives from Leo Burnett Advertising, I sat in a conference room with some of Procter & Gamble's most savvy marketing honchos. We viewed five commercials we had produced for a new product. All five took radically different approaches, so we knew that one would test higher than the others; there would not be a five-way tie. Among ourselves, we each picked the one we thought would be the winner.

Here we had four members of one of America's most successful advertising agencies and five high-level management types from one of America's most successful mass-market manufacturers. Of the nine of us, none picked the winner.

It goes to show that when it comes to marketing, you can't go on judgment alone. You've just got to experiment. Sometimes these experiments will cost money. Other times, they'll cost time. But they'll always be worth both.

To a guerrilla, even one who is strapped for cash, it shouldn't matter whether a marketing weapon is free or costs money. The main consideration is whether the weapon produces results. Still, I know that while I'm snuggled between the cozy pages of a book, you're out there in the real world—definitely under fire from competitors, and possibly so strapped for cash that it does matter whether or not a marketing weapon is free.

For you, here is a list of 50 guerrilla marketing weapons that are free.

1. Name
2. Niche
3. Color
4. Theme
5. Research studies
6. Marketing plan
7. Identity
8. Pricing
9. Customer mailing list
10. Attire
11. Phone demeanor
12. Neatness
13. Smiles
14. Speed
15. Service
16. Follow-up
17. Contact time with the customer
18. How you say hello and good-bye
19. Publicity contacts
20. Brand-name awareness
21. Enthusiasm
22. Competitiveness
23. Community involvement
24. Window displays
25. Club and association memberships
26. Sales training
27. Books and articles

28. Courses and lectures
29. Gift certificates
30. Testimonials
31. Tie-ins with others
32. Hours of operation
33. Days of operation
34. Availability of financing
35. Credibility
36. Satisfied customers
37. Word-of-mouth
38. Public relations
39. Telemarketing scripts
40. Access to co-op funds
41. Access to marketing materials
42. Column in a publication
43. Special events
44. Seminars and workshops
45. Merchandise displays
46. Demonstrations
47. Consultations
48. Sales presentations
49. Sales representatives
50. Reputation

If you want to be a nitpicker, you can claim that some of these do cost money. But I am armed with antinitpicking logic and can prove that none has to cost money.

The other 50, the ones that do cost money, may cost far less than you think. For example, although a reprint of a publicity story may cost just a nickel, I concede that it does cost money and have not included it on my list of free weapons.

This book is both a marketing book and a kind of reference book. To get the most from it, I suggest that you read it just as you'd read any other book—front to back. Later, you can treat it as a reference book by referring to weapons about which you want further information.

Readers of my past books know it is crucial that you always remember the eight secrets of success in guerrilla marketing—eight words that end in the letters *ent* and represent eight ideas by which your company must live. The 100 weapons won't even have the punch of a cap gun if you don't live by these eight principles:

1. *Commitment:* This is what makes marketing work; if you won't commit to it, it may not work for you.
2. *Investment:* Though it feels like an expense, marketing funds are really investments, good ones.

3. *Consistent:* Allow your audience to become familiar with your identity and benefits by staying the course.
4. *Confident:* A national survey proved that the factor that most affects sales is consumer trust; people patronize businesses in which they are confident.
5. *Patient:* You can practice commitment, think of marketing as an investment, be consistent, and make prospects confident only if you are patient.
6. *Assortment:* Marketing is not advertising or direct mail; it's a broad assortment of weaponry.
7. *Subsequent:* Nonguerrillas think marketing is over when they've made the sale. Guerrillas know the profits come from what they do subsequent to the sale.
8. *Convenient:* Now, more than ever, it is crucial that you are easy to buy from, easy to do business with.

Memorize these words; live by these concepts. Then expect your guerrilla marketing weapons to work their wonders for your bottom line.

2

WEAPONS FOR THE OUTSET

The Boy Scouts aren't the only group that knows the importance of being prepared. Guerrilla marketers know very well the necessity of having their marketing weapons at the ready, their tools all set to manufacture new customers from day one.

Guerrillas also know that some very important marketing weapons will be useless to them until the companies are off and running. They know that other weapons must come to the fore at the outset. This chapter examines those weapons.

If yours is a company that has been sailing along the sea of profitability for aeons and aeons, you certainly have given these weapons their due regard. But if yours is a company that is brand new, relatively new, or even an established company that is just getting around to launching a proper marketing program, these are the weapons upon which you must concentrate.

First things first, and these are the first of the first. Your name is probably the very first marketing weapon that will capture the attention of your public. No company would open without first deciding its name, right? Well, usually right, but not always. There have been companies that were so enthusiastic about their offerings that they actually ran ads with the offers, ads that had their prices clearly printed and even listed their address. But the ads didn't include the name of the company. An oversight? Worse. The company never came up with a moniker for itself. Surely you have one. The data on names will help you decide if it's a good or a bad name.

Names are easier than niches. Your name will set you apart from all other companies on planet Earth. Your niche will set you apart from your competition. It will tell exactly what you stand for. And you've got to know it before you do business rather than figure it out later, while you're wondering why the competition is clobbering you.

If you don't have a clearly understandable niche yet, you should by the time you complete this chapter.

Quality is another weapon of the guerrilla. By this time, I'm sure you've figured that guerrilla marketing is not a shuck-and-jive show. Instead, it's a way of promoting honest quality. In fact, if you offer poor quality, guerrilla marketing will hasten the day that your company closes its doors because more people will learn of that lack of quality sooner than otherwise.

Although I may be stating the obvious, I must alert you that your product or service must be redolent of quality before guerrilla marketing should even be mentioned, before you even get a user's license for your weaponry. High quality, therefore, is an omnipotent weapon for the outset and forever after. It will serve as the cornerstone for your reputation, your mass marketing, your word-of-mouth advertising, your very existence. Without that high quality, you may as well face up to the fact that perhaps you're not cut out to be a guerrilla. Fast hands and a glib tongue will not help you succeed. High quality and guerrilla marketing: That's the ticket to success. Once you have the quality, you have a prime qualification to be a guerrilla.

This chapter will also talk about color. Although you may not realize it, most companies end up with a color, so it's better to select it at the outset. This color may manifest itself on your business card, stationery, signs, brochures, logo, any of a number of places. Needless to say, but I'll say it anyhow because of its importance, the color will influence the unconscious minds of your prospects, where purchase decisions are made. You won't want an orange business card, a pink sign, and a blue logo. Pretty as that may sound, a single color will work more to your advantage.

A logo or symbol of your company will also prove advantageous because it offers a visual representation of your company. With so many small businesses being launched, you want to give your prospects all the help they need to recall you. A logo provides that help. You need one before you start doing business if you're to be a guerrilla. Learn of logos by reading of them right here.

This chapter will tell you a thing or two about theme lines as well. If you don't want a theme line, you've got to change that thinking, because your prospects need all they can possibly get just to remember you, let alone patronize your business. A theme line will help in that regard.

Some misguided businesspeople think that location, another weapon for the outset, is the name of the profit game. But Jay Conrad Levinson is here to tell you that if you put all your hopes in your location and ignore the other weapons of guerrilla marketing, you will be missing ninety-nine boats as they sail off into the sunset of success. Location is often very important. But it is hardly all there is to marketing. Otherwise a real estate agent would be writing this book.

Research studies are very valuable to guerrillas, more at the outset than anytime else because they help so much in strategic planning. In this chapter, you'll learn where to get your hands on those studies. You'll also learn that the more places people can buy what you sell, the more money you will earn. The word for this is *distribution*, and it is a potent weapon—or a wimpy weapon, depending on your product, your service, and your personality. We'll give distribution due attention in this chapter.

Attention is similarly due a marketing plan. My past books show how to create a simple, seven-sentence plan. This chapter will do the same. Entering business without such a plan is like entering a battle under a commander who shouts, "Ready . . . fire . . . aim!"

If you've read either of my other guerrilla marketing books or heard me speak at a seminar, you know that I detest the idea of a company *image*, the very suggestion of which conjures up phoniness and visions of customers sensing you've misrepresented yourself. You know that I prefer, even demand, that businesses portray their *identity*, because it is automatically honest. You'll need to deeply understand that identity, just as you require self-knowledge to be happy in today's world—and tomorrow's as well. But worry not. Information is forthcoming.

A pricing policy is still another weapon for the outset rather than something you figure out as you go along. Winning companies are not reactive, but instead cause others to react to them. This happens when you have a pricing policy. It does not when you do not. Discuss that policy before opening your doors. Maybe you'll change it later; that's OK. But it's not OK to be hazy on your pricing.

Nearing the end of the weapons you need for the outset, we come to selection, one of the most important factors in attracting prospects and winning new customers. These people want a selection; study after study proves it. Get ready to offer it before you commence your operations, or many people, important ones, will get the wrong idea about your company. You never want that to happen.

Finally, and I saved this for the end because I want to stress its importance, is your customer mailing list. At the very outset, it has zero names on it. At the end of one day, it has several names on it. At the end of one year, it has many names on it. At the end of three years, it is perhaps your most precious marketing weapon and most valuable business asset.

I urge you to consider it as a weapon for the outset because so many otherwise intelligent business owners don't begin compiling this list until they are a few years old. Don't make such a ridiculous error. Start your list the first day. And read the words about it that are about to come your way.

If you haven't yet spent time thinking about these 14 weapons for the outset, consider yourself fortunate to begin thinking of them now. Self-respecting guerrillas, exactly how I hope to describe you, have these weapons armed and ready to use in the good fight for sales. Lucky for you, some business owners never get around to figuring them out.

NAME

The name of a business exerts a powerful influence over the prospects for the products or service offered by the business. In general, rules governing a business name are:

1. Be sure it has absolutely no negative connotations.
2. Make it easy to pronounce and spell.
3. Try to use a name that will not result in any confusion, such as a name that looks or sounds like an existing name.
4. Don't name a company in a way that limits expansion. Acme Sleep Shop means you'll always sell sleep products or have to change your name. Acme Interiors is more open to expansion.
5. Try to find a name that describes your business, such as Jiffy Auto Lube. Note that this name also conveys a benefit.
6. Avoid trendy names like the plague. When the trend dies out, your business may do the same.
7. Attempt to convey your identity with your name: dignity, largeness, local identification, quality, whatever.
8. Use of your own name is usually a good hedge against infringing on someone else's name.
9. Ask: How will my name sound on the phone? On the radio? What will it look like in ads? On stationery?
10. If your business might attract prospects from the yellow pages, use a name that will be listed first. Aardvark?

There is no rule that says a business name must be cutesy-pie, though some names lead you to believe such a rule exists. There is also no rule that dictates your name must say what your business is all about. Some successful businesses keep their names vague so that they can engage in several activities. Peter Handler and Associates is an example of this.

It is always a good idea to have a lawyer subject any name you might select to a name search—just to be sure you are stepping on no toes. Few things are more disturbing than having to change your business name after you've hit it big. Yet, only then will someone come down on you for infringement.

Recognize that some successful names suggest a logo (Apple); others suggest absolutely nothing (Exxon); still others are named after the founder (Benetton). In general, names that are the owner's have a smidgeon more credibility. Incidentally, many names are selected strictly for their credibility (General Dynamics).

When considering what to name your business, the bottom line is that there are many wonderful names and many terrible names. Your job is not necessarily to select the best name, but to pick any one of the wonderful names and avoid the terrible ones.

Here's one that gives a benefit, stands apart, and is unique: Guerrilla Marketing International. The only problem is that on the phone it sounds like "Gorilla Marketing International." Good thing we don't depend on the phone for our customers.

NICHE

Unless you have absolutely no competition now and never will have any, you're well-advised to select a niche that differentiates your business from all competitors.

The niche can be quality or service, speed or convenience, experience or low prices, innovation or selection, or any other attribute for which you wish to be known. Just realize that before you obtain a healthy share of market you're going to have to obtain a healthy share of mind. And the selection of a unique and desirable niche is a smart place to begin.

Naturally, the niche should be one that is a natural benefit offered by your business. So if you are a high-priced consultant or run a high-line retail store, you probably shouldn't consider low prices as a niche.

In choosing your niche, keep three factors in mind:

1. Your competition
2. Your target audience
3. Your own operation

The idea is to pick a niche that fits in well with all three. All of your marketing should create a deeper and deeper connection between your company and your niche. Sure, you can choose to stand for high quality while still promoting your service and your selection. But you've got to communicate the idea of high quality with all your marketing ammunition—from your stationery to your yellow page ads, from your direct-mail letters to your sales presentations.

In all those marketing vehicles, high quality should leap into the mind of your prospect. When prospects and customers think of your company, they should think of high quality. And, of course, you should offer high quality.

If you don't pick a clear and meaningful niche, you'll end

up standing for nothing. This makes you easy pickings for any competitor. On the other hand, when you give serious thought to your niche, you can gain a powerful competitive advantage.

Many successful companies study their markets looking for unoccupied niches. That's where they hang their marketing hats. These companies realize that many product and service categories are vulnerable in areas that no one has claimed. So they claim the turf for themselves. And they do what is necessary to live up to their niche.

Since your niche governs so much of your marketing, it deserves careful scrutiny. And always consider moving into a niche that a competitor occupies if you can do a better job of filling it.

The buzzword for niche is *positioning*. Whatever you call it, just be sure you know it and communicate it.

Quality

I'm amazed when I meet clients who have everything all set, except for the high quality of their products. They begin their marketing, people buy their products, and then their world begins to crumble.

Their poor quality results in dissatisfied customers. Their aggressive marketing attracts a lot of these people—all unhappy with the quality of either the product or the service. Sounds as if a first-grader could have avoided the problem. Trouble is, some businesspeople have less sense than a first-grader.

Do all that you can to ensure the high quality of whatever it is that you are selling. If you find a flaw, don't do any marketing. Remember, guerrilla marketing works only if you offer high quality. Otherwise, guerrilla marketing speeds the demise of your business because so many people learn of it so quickly.

If the high quality is there, the profits will be there. If the high quality is absent, today's equivalent of debtor's prison will open its doors for you.

Once you have the high quality and the quality control to be sure that absolutely everything you sell is of unimpeachable quality, then you have a valuable and hardworking weapon. That high quality is your weapon. It will enable you to compare your offerings with those of your competition. It will allow you to justify your pricing. It will enhance your word-of-mouth marketing. It will serve as the fodder for all of your marketing materials.

In a study conducted to determine which factors most influence sales, quality came in second—right after confidence in the seller. If you think that means you must concentrate on your quality, you're thinking like a guerrilla.

Many firms understand the importance of high quality, but do not realize that it is a weapon of marketing. They assume people automatically figure they will offer high quality. But this is not true. People have been disappointed in the quality of items they have purchased in many instances. They need your marketing to reassure them that the high quality will be there when they purchase from you.

I feel almost silly telling you so basic a fact. But I tell it because I have seen so many otherwise smart businesspeople fall flat on their dreams because they relegated quality to a lesser position than they should have.

Marketing, they knew, is what moves goods. This may be true, but it moves goods only once. High quality leads to repeat and referral sales. And these are the wellsprings of profits.

COLOR

While it is true that many businesses can thrive and prosper in black and white, many others require a specific color or colors to win the battle for the customer.

Perhaps you'll have to go into the complexity of full color, utilizing all the hues of the rainbow and then some. But it's more likely that you'll want to become associated with a single color.

The reason for this is to gain a firmer foothold in the minds of your prospects. And without a share of your prospects' minds, you'll have a tougher time gaining a share of the market in which you plan to flourish.

Coca-Cola's company color is red. It's on their signs, on their cans, in their ads. McDonald's arches are synonymous with golden (as are their corporate profits).

Your color may make itself known, even if you engage in no advertising, with your business cards, stationery, newsletter, vans, sign, logo, brochures, perhaps even with your office. And that color will help implant your company's identity in the unconscious minds of your prospects.

What's the right color for you?

Well, it's not the color your competitors are using, unless you intentionally want to get in on their action. Blue is a color never associated with food. Green is a color often associated with anything natural. Pink is feminine. Gray is masculine. Maroon is not equated with low prices. Neither is gold. But red is a color that goes well with low prices.

According to some psychologists specializing in color, there are four basic colors (dark blue, blue-green, orange-red, and bright yellow) plus four auxiliary colors (violet, brown, black, and neutral gray).

Dark blue, they say, represents depth of feeling, signifying tranquillity, contentment, tenderness, and love/affection. Blue-green represents elasticity of will, signifying persistence, self-assertion, obstinacy, and self-esteem. Orange-red represents force of will, signifying desire, excitability, domination, and sexuality. And bright yellow represents spontaneity, signifying variability, expectancy, originality, and exhilaration. Of the auxiliary colors, black, gray, and brown are thought to indicate a negative attitude. Violet indicates taste and graciousness.

The color you choose should tie in with the niche and identity you choose. Then again, you may choose to deprive your company of the psychological impact of a color. For your sake and the sake of your future customers, I hope you become associated with at least one color.

Logo

Because so many people are visually oriented, a guerrilla-minded company will always have a logotype—a distinctive symbol—to aid in identifying their company.

With a logo, visually stimulated people are more apt to remember the company as well as respond to its marketing. This is why it is always a good idea to use your logo whenever possible: in your advertising, on your package or sign, on your stationery and business card, on your order forms and invoices, and anywhere else possible. The more places the better—because of the synergistic action.

The cost to create a logo runs as high as $50,000—not an unusual price for a Fortune 500 company to pay—down to $250. It can even be free—if you can design or select a preexisting design element at a local printer.

There are five important things to remember when a logo is designed for your company:

1. It should be able to function as your logo for twenty years or more. The repetition will serve you well.
2. It should be simple and easy to understand, and should not confuse people in any way.
3. It should not be suggestive of the logo of another company, to be clear and to avoid potential litigation.
4. It should be compatible with your name, identity, visual format, and future plans.
5. It should be clearly discernible whether it is one yard square or one-half inch square.

If you might ever use television in your marketing, and I hope you might, consider the aptness of the logo to motion, animation, color, and live action. Might it be an integral part of your commercial or merely tacked on at the end?

It is necessary that your logo be approved first in a

black-and-white version—since it will sometimes appear that way regardless of your selection of colors. Newspaper ads are rarely in color, and yellow pages ads permit red only—for now.

Guerrillas do all in their power to motivate people, to access the unconscious minds of their prospects, to outmarket the competition. A logo is one more weapon that aids them in all these quests.

Be sure you have a logo, and do all in your power, by using it wherever and whenever you can, to ensure that it will attract new customers and profits for you now and well into the next century. If you have no logo, you're not a guerrilla.

THEME

A theme is a set of words that summarizes your identity, benefits, or uniqueness. The best themes are those that can be utilized for decades. The longer you use them, the more powerful they become.

You've heard of the power of a brand name? One of the ways to get one is to give people a theme to remember you by. Some of the best themes in the land have been around for twenty years, even fifty years. They're the best because they're as fresh the day you read this as they were when they were invented. And the companies that use them are bigger today than the day they first used them.

A few examples:

"You're in good hands with Allstate."
"Fly the friendly skies of United."
". . . in the valley of the jolly—ho-ho-ho—Green Giant."
"The Maytag repairman is the loneliest man in town."
"Come to Marlboro Country."
"Tastes great. Less filling."

I could go on—and so could you—but you get the point. The idea of a theme is permanence. Themes are not to be changed around or else they are wordplay rather than marketing themes. Wordplay doesn't win nearly as many customers as a marketing theme.

Where does a practicing guerrilla use a marketing theme? The answer: in as many places as possible. On brochures, in ads, in commercials, on business cards, on signs, at trade shows, in letters, anywhere he or she can.

Don't forget: Themes, like wines, cheeses, and my wife, improve with age.

Themes should not contain trendy words or they'll become old-fashioned when the word goes out of style. Themes should not be long-winded; strive for brevity. Themes should suggest a visual element so that they may be brought to life by graphics. Themes should be created with both the present and the future in mind. Don't theme yourself into a corner by saying you're "A Great Little Stereo Shop" when two years from now you'll also be featuring video.

In a decade that is seeing more new businesses launched than any other decade in history, the competition is becoming both plentiful and sophisticated. Only the companies that develop a brand-name awareness will survive and prosper. You are reading, here and now, about one more way to get that kind of awareness.

If you don't have a theme now, get one. If you have one, lean on it. You'll find it to be a potent weapon.

Location

Although real estate experts will tell you that the three primary factors in selecting real estate are location, location, and location, a marketing expert would say otherwise.

A guerrilla marketing expert would extol the benefits of a convenient location, but that same expert would alert you to the fact that location is but one one-hundredth of a well-stocked guerrilla marketing arsenal, and that in many cases it is far from the most important weapon.

The criteria for selecting a great location are:

1. It is convenient to your target market.
2. It offers ample parking for all who might visit you.
3. It fits with your marketing identity.
4. It is on your prospects' way home, on the way to your prospects' offices, or on the way to something that makes it simple for prospects to visit.
5. It is easy to find.
6. It offers good visibility, good lighting, a spacious window for displays, a sane landlord, and compatible neighbors.
7. It attracts walk-by or drive-by traffic.
8. It does not have prohibitive sign restrictions.
9. It is large enough for all your needs.
10. You can afford it without busting your budget.

Don't make the mistake of paying a huge rent or purchase price for a location if yours is a business that is not dependent on a high-traffic location. These days people will drive out of their way for great values. Still, accessibility to major thoroughfares and public transportation is often a plus.

Recognize that even the finest location can only get people into your door, store, or office. Many a bankrupt entrepreneur banked everything on location only to fall flat on his or her entrepreneurial derriere because no other aspects of marketing were properly attended to.

Factors influencing location are whether your prospects will be walking or driving, whether they will ever visit your place of business, whether your suppliers are nearby, and whether you can make the leasehold improvements you desire.

If yours is a tough-to-find location and people will be visiting you, be sure you include a simple map in your marketing materials. When giving your location, mention the address, the cross street, and any nearby landmarks. Location can, I'll admit, be the making or breaking of many a business. But it is hardly ever the only factor.

If your location is a good one, don't neglect your other 99 weapons.

RESEARCH STUDIES

Obviously, the more information you have, the more accurately you can aim your marketing weapons. The information you require gives you knowledge about your prospects, customers, competition, media, local economy, and your market.

You can obtain this information from several sources. Some are completely free; others are costly, but worth it if the information they provide can be used to gain sales.

Let's examine a few of your options. You'll probably want to exercise several of them:

1. You can design your own questionnaire, asking customers or prospects a host of questions. As long as you keep the whole thing anonymous and if you explain that you require the information so as to be of better service and offer better quality, you can ask many questions, gain many answers, learn crucial data about how to market your offerings with the deadly effectiveness of a guerrilla.

2. You can access data banks with your computer, modem, and telephone. Existing studies are already there. All that's required is for you to connect up with them.

3. You can gain important information about your market and competition from a good public library. Reference librarians are among the nation's most precious untapped resources. Tell them what you're looking for and just watch them find it.

4. Contact your local chamber of commerce and ask to see their market studies. They'll have an impressive amount. And the cost to you will probably be nil.

5. Get in touch with associations within your industry, requesting their own research studies. These may cost a bit, but will be especially valuable since they were conducted or financed by others in your own industry.

6. Write to the publications that serve your industry, requesting their own market studies. Chances are good that they'll have a wealth of information.

7. Get in touch with a reputable research organization. A company such as Q.E.D. Research, Inc., at 415-932-3202, can help you find out virtually anything you want— anything.

8. Ask for research studies available from marketing publications such as *Adweek,* 213-937-4330, or *Advertising Age*, 312-649-5200. The more you learn, the more you earn.

9. Call University Microfilms at 800-521-0600 and you'll have access to one million Ph.D. dissertations. Certainly at least one of them can impart crucial information to you.

Distribution

Distribution refers to the places where your product or service may be purchased. In general, the wider your distribution, the greater your sales. However, savvy guerrillas focus more on the quality of their distribution outlets than on the quantity.

They are extremely careful not to invest marketing money or energy where they do not have distribution. For instance, if the city of Phoenix clamored for your product because they saw it on "The Tonight Show," but your product wasn't available in Phoenix, you'd be out of luck—in Phoenix, at least.

Businesses gain distribution by means of their own sales forces, which sell to outlets throughout the marketing area; by means of independent sales reps, who sell other items along with those of the business hiring them, generally paying a commission on sales ranging from 15 percent to 40 percent; or by working with an existing distribution organization whose sole function is to gain distribution and continue to add new outlets while calling on established outlets.

Again, having ten ordinary distributors isn't nearly as effective as working with five first-class distributors. You can tell the first-class organizations by their number of accounts, number of sales reps, number of times they call on existing customers, and by asking for the lowdown on them from some of their clients.

Many businesses prosper with absolutely no distribution outlets. They utilize the power of direct marketing and sell their wares via direct mail, telemarketing, postcard decks, coupon ads, take-one brochures, direct-response TV, home-shopping shows, and catalogs—to name but a few methods of getting around a poor system of distribution.

Although many businesses set a goal to establish many

distribution outlets, others steer away from them, preferring to keep the 15 percent to 40 percent for themselves.

Your product is often judged by the places at which it is distributed. You'd feel differently about a product available at Tiffany's than you would about one available at a discount drugstore. You'd feel more confident in the Tiffany product. And confidence wins customers.

These days, with so many chain operations, it is possible to establish several hundred distribution outlets through just one monumental effort with one company. If your product, or service, can be sold at these chain outlets, there's a good chance you can gain national, even international, distribution via this method.

But always remember that the bottom line is your bottom line.

MARKETING PLAN

This marketing weapon costs nary a cent, guides all your efforts down the most propitious path, and yet is absent from the arsenals of most businesses.

Why does this happen? Probably because most business owners are intimidated by the mere topic of marketing. Because they aren't certain what it's all about, they market by ear, making up their campaigns as they go along, acting on the advice of diverse sources, and shunning the act of putting their plans down in writing.

Worse, some of them employ firms to create marketing plans. The marketing companies, seeking to justify their probably lofty prices, submit plans with heft and mass—long, ungainly booklets that only serve to intimidate the business owner further.

A good marketing plan intimidates no one, except perhaps the competition. It serves as a written map of the route—showing the goal and how to attain it. To keep it understandable, it should be brief. This improves the focus. Without focus, marketing is a waste of money.

Guerrillas have long been able to operate from a seven-sentence marketing plan. Here are the seven sentences and an example of how a small bookstore put them to good use:

1. One sentence tells the purpose of your marketing.
   "THE PURPOSE OF PAGE ONE BOOKSTORE MARKETING IS TO BUILD AN INCREASING BASE OF REPEAT CUSTOMERS."

2. One sentence tells how this purpose will be achieved, focusing upon the benefits of your offering.
   "THIS WILL BE ACHIEVED BY STRESSING THE SELECTION OF BOOK AND NONBOOK ITEMS WITHIN THE STORE."

3. One sentence defines your target audience.
   "OUR TARGET AUDIENCE IS BOOK-BUYING ADULT FE-

MALES WITHIN A ONE-MILE RADIUS OF PAGE ONE BOOK-
STORE."

4. One sentence describes proposed marketing vehicles.
"MARKETING VEHICLES TO BE EMPLOYED WILL INCLUDE
NEWSPAPER ADS RUN WEEKLY IN THREE PAPERS, A WIN-
DOW DISPLAY THAT CHANGES WEEKLY, NUMEROUS SIGNS
INSIDE THAT MERCHANDISE AND CROSS-MERCHANDISE,
A YELLOW PAGES AD, QUARTERLY AUTOGRAPH PAR-
TIES, QUARTERLY AUTHOR LECTURES, QUARTERLY IN-
STORE SEMINARS, FM RADIO ADVERTISING, POSTCARD
MAILINGS EVERY TWO MONTHS, BROCHURES, A CATA-
LOG, A ONE-TIME MAGAZINE AD, TIE-INS WITH ALL LO-
CAL CONFERENCES, ACCESSING CO-OP FUNDS, AND USE
OF OUR MARKETING THEME ON BAGS, BOOKMARKS, IN-
VOICES, GIFT CERTIFICATES, AND GIFTS."

5. One sentence tells about your niche in the market.
"PAGE ONE'S NICHE WILL BE A CAREFUL SELECTION
TAILORED FOR THE COMMUNITY."

6. One sentence gives your identity.
"OUR IDENTITY WILL BE PORTRAYED AS WARM, HONEST,
KNOWLEDGEABLE, UP-TO-DATE, AND ULTRAFRIENDLY,
AS EVIDENCED BY OUR GREETING PEOPLE BY NAME,
TAKING PHONE ORDERS, SETTING UP CHARGE ACCOUNTS,
SHIPPING ANYWHERE IN THE WORLD, AND DOING FREE
GIFT WRAPPING."

7. One sentence describes your marketing budget ex-
pressed as a percent of your projected gross sales.
"10 PERCENT OF PROJECTED GROSS SALES WILL BE DE-
VOTED TO MARKETING."

Any business can create a seven-sentence marketing plan
such as this one. Each year it should be reviewed, and each
marketing decision should be judged by whether it fulfills
the promises inherent within the plan.
If you want, you can add one hundred pages of docu-

mentation. If you want, you can winnow it down to seven words to hone your focus even more. Page One might put it like this: "WE WILL BE THE QUINTESSENTIAL COMMUNITY BOOKSTORE." Operating without a marketing plan is akin to driving a car with the windows painted over, no brakes, and no steering wheel. Don't try it.

IDENTITY

A word to strike from your marketing vocabulary is *image*. An image is a façade, something phony. People sit in a room and try to decide what image to portray. They come up with all sorts of high-falutin characteristics, then communicate these as part of their image. Unfortunately, the whole thing backfires.

Prospects come in or order or phone and learn that the company is not, indeed, what it held itself out to be in the first place. Instead, it is different—not bad, but different.

This makes the prospect unconsciously feel ripped off. The prospect was victimized by your misrepresentation of yourself because you communicated an image that had little basis in reality, only in hope.

A far better *i* word than image is *identity*. An identity is automatically honest. If you communicate your real identity, people feel a sense of relaxation when they contact you because they see, again on an unconscious level, that you are exactly who you portrayed yourself to be.

They know that you did not misrepresent your personality, so they are more likely to believe other things you say. It is not always simple to come up with your identity, but it is always possible.

Get a few people in your operation plus one or two objective parties to list words that describe your identity. Be honest with yourself. Then try to convey that identity in all of your marketing materials. It won't be difficult because it's real. People will feel a sense of connectedness with you because they trusted you and you did not, unlike many other businesses, betray that trust.

As you steer clear of anything that even hints at an image, you should veer toward everything that proves your identity. Be sure your ads, brochures, windows, letters, wording, graphics, office, salespeople, telephone demeanor, and employees reflect that identity. It will make your customers feel good. They enjoy an honest personality, and by conveying yours, you are giving your customers what they want and what they unconsciously need.

If you have been marketing an image up till now, begin now to switch over to marketing your identity, to being completely honest in your communications. Remove the whole concept of image from your marketing. Regardless of what you'd like to be, if you're not it yet, don't act as though you are. That's really the essence of identity.

You'll find the entire marketing process gets a bit easier once you have embraced the idea of communicating your identity.

PRICING

Because guerrilla marketing is so dedicated to profits, it considers pricing to be a foremost marketing element. This is not to say it recommends a high price or a low price. I have seen both fail miserably.

Instead, it means a price that delivers to you a fair profit. It also means a competitive price. People are very price conscious; I don't have to tell you that. But I do have to tell you that only 14 percent of people consider price to be the prime influence over a sale.

In a research study designed to show the prime influences, confidence came in first, quality came in second, service came in third, and selection came in fourth; price came in ninth. Only 14 percent of the people surveyed placed price at number one. This also means 86 percent found factors more important than price. Price is important. But there are many considerations that are more important.

When pricing, first and always consider the cost of the goods to you and the worth of your time. Then consider your competition and your target audience. It's always a good idea to develop a pricing strategy so that you carve out your own niche in the marketplace—or at least fit into a niche that can prove profitable to you.

One such niche may be at the top of the mass-market premium-priced brands. Another might be to be lower than any local competition. Still a third might be to sell all items and services at exactly double what they cost you.

People are far more interested in *value* than price. Because of that, you can make your products or services available at high market prices, which decrease considerably with volume purchases. This can do wonders for your bottom line if you keep overall profit in mind at all times.

Unfortunately (or fortunately, depending on your outlook), almost everybody wants a good deal. So be prepared to lower your price if that is standard in your industry. Be prepared to market your offerings at sale prices.

But beware; having sales is the heroin of business. It is pleasurable, addictive, and dangerous. If you feel you must have sales, refrain from heralding them in all your marketing or else your prospects will wait until you have a sale before buying.

Some unwise nonguerrillas have been known to break all their sales records by adding free merchandise to all purchased merchandise, only to learn that they lost money in the process. As in all guerrilla marketing, let profits guide your decisions. And the more you can think long term versus short term, the happier you'll be in the end.

Selection

Everyone wants a choice. And the larger the choice, the better. The fact is, only consumer confidence, quality, and service rate more important than selection as factors influencing why people patronize one business over another.

Your selection need not merely be large. It can be the biggest selection of subgroups, such as laptop computers, imported fabrics, or colors. The idea is that you have a vast range of components in which you can offer selection.

Some businesses offer items at a selection of prices, from high to low. Others offer only high-priced items, but with a large selection of styles. And still others might offer only low-priced items, but with a big selection of related items.

If you have gone to great lengths to provide a wide selection, make this clear in your marketing. Perhaps you traveled to enlarge your selection. Possibly you made special buys. Alert your prospects to the lengths you have gone simply to provide a generous selection.

Even if you offer services, you can find ways to provide a selection. Instead of a one-time project, maybe you can also make available three-time projects, yearlong projects, or monthly projects.

The mere offering of a selection makes it easier for salespeople to sell and customers to buy. The selection gives the salesperson a place to close the sale: "Would you like it in oak or teak?"

Allow your marketing to convey your selection both verbally and visually. The more you emphasize your selection, the more likely your prospect will be to decide you've got exactly what he or she wants.

If you're a manufacturer, you'll find that retailers will appreciate your selection because it can give them more shelf facings, increasing the value of your entire display, and, further, proving their comprehensiveness as a retail establishment. You gain. The store gains. The customer gains.

The ideal situation is to provide your prospects and customers with a selection of selections—many areas where they have several options. As the prospect decides among the options, important momentum toward the sale is created. In addition, the buyer is very probably going to find exactly what will offer the maximum purchase satisfaction.

Frequently, the only difference between the success and the failure is the breadth or quality of their selections. But remember, along with selection, you must exercise superb taste.

CUSTOMER MAILING LIST

Do everything short of illegal activities to compile a gigantic and loyal mailing list of people who have purchased from you. Obtain this list by:

1. Having a sign-up book in your store
2. Automatically adding the names of all your customers
3. Asking your salespeople to secure names for the list
4. All of the above

You can enlarge the list, though not with bona fide customers, by having contests or sweepstakes in which people must write their names and addresses in order to enter.

Once you've gotten a customer list, and this is one of the few times I strongly urge you to do this, put it into a computer; recognize deep in your heart that the list is worth far more than its weight in gold.

These are very special people. They know who you are, where you are, what it is like to do business with you. For your sake, I hope your customers are satisfied.

Satisfy them by keeping in touch with them on a regular basis. Invite them to special sales. Let them in on special events, news, bargains, shipments. Remember their birthdays or at least do something at Christmas. Valentine's Day would be a neat holiday to remember them. I tell you this because I want you to love them.

If you do, you will treat them like the kind of people who grace your life with repeat sales and then more repeat sales. They refer your business to friends, neighbors, associates.

Bless these folks on your long (I hope) customer list, because they are the mouths from which the words flow in word-of-mouth advertising. Do you think a total stranger is going to talk you up?

Your customer mailing list should be kept up-to-date, clean, guarded, and in a fireproof container. The list can be rented to others for cash. You can do that over and over and over. Just call people listed under "mailing lists" in your yellow pages.

The wisest of the guerrilla marketers invest 10 percent of their marketing funds toward attracting the universe, which is everyone who could possibly be exposed to their marketing; 30 percent toward attracting their prospects, who are those people with the greatest proclivity to buy; and 60 percent toward attracting their customers, who contribute the greatest source of profits. This is a superb way of increasing sales while decreasing marketing costs. If that's not Nirvana, what is?

3

WEAPONS NOT RECOGNIZED AS PART OF MARKETING

Many companies bemoan their inability to afford marketing, yet engage in business practices daily that they don't realize are actually, when viewed through the keen eyes of a guerrilla, marketing weapons indeed.

Still other firms are unaware of the weaponry available to them. This lack of awareness stems from the fact that the weapons are either too new to be at the forefront of the marketing chief's mind or too old to be taken seriously. By not recognizing the potency of these weapons—and not even understanding that they have anything at all to do with marketing—these firms are depriving themselves of marketing power, not to mention sales and profits.

Of the 100 guerrilla marketing weapons, 16 fit neatly into the category of weapons not recognized as weapons.

I begin with the package because some people think they don't have one since they don't have any boxes sitting on supermarket shelves. But all companies have a package, whether it's a store, an office, a sales rep, or a carton that sits on a supermarket shelf.

Next, I want to call your attention to the business card, which is right out of the 1950s if all it has is your name, address, and telephone number. Hardly a marketing weapon if it's used only in that way.

Stationery is also covered because it's another of the multitude of tiny impressions that you make upon your buying public. I certainly won't kid you and say that people look at your stationery and think, "Boy, this is such gorgeous stationery, I'll go out and buy the product today!" People also don't see your stationery and think, "Yuck! Such poorly designed stationery. You'll never catch me buying what *they* sell." Life doesn't work like that. But life does work with prospects making purchase or no-purchase decisions based on many little details. And your stationery is one of those details. It's your choice: a marketing opportunity or a lost opportunity.

Most business owners give little thought to their order forms, invoices, receipts, and other business paperwork. But guerrillas recognize the marketing potential of these, and so will you once you've completed Chapter 3.

Inserts, also known as preprints, are rapidly being discovered as freeways to profit. The trouble is, only the big guys are discovering them, and I want the little guys to know about them, too, so they're included in this chapter. That may turn out to be the best business news you've come across in a long, long time. I certainly hope so.

The chapter also alerts you to contests and sweepstakes because I realize most readers don't know the dynamite marketing potential of these. It's more than a free trip to Las Vegas or wherever. It's the key to a mailing list that acts like a gold mine.

If you were a farmer, you'd know that roadside stands are great places to sell fresh produce. If you were a guerrilla, you'd know they're profitable distribution centers for a lot more than sweet corn.

Gift baskets are usually associated with department stores. So I stuck them smack dab in the middle of Chapter 3 to call your attention to them—knowing full well that you're no department store. But you're an open-minded business-person interested in turning an honest profit. Speaking of profits, there are those who consider their pursuit to be a vice. Guerrillas feel exactly the opposite, sensing correctly that the real vice is operating at a loss rather than a profit.

You'd think that audiovisual aids definitely are recognized as part of marketing. But if this were so, more businesses would employ them. So few businesses do use them, let alone use them properly, that I'm confident most firms are oblivious to them and to the wonders they work when it comes to converting prospects into paying customers.

Almost everyone knows about brochures. But hardly anyone is aware that audiotapes and videotapes are electronic brochures, and are more likely to penetrate the mind of a prospect than a standard nonelectronic brochure.

These days, when you phone a business, there's a good chance you'll be put on hold, aptly nicknamed "permahold" by my wife. To alleviate the permahold situation, it is now possible to end consumer resentment and increase sales by employing marketing-on-phone-hold. Never heard of it? I didn't think so. That's why I've included it.

Your decor is an important part of your operation. But did you also know it is a marketing weapon? Guerrillas are fully aware that it is, and they decorate their stores or offices with the increasing of sales in mind.

Whoever thought that the clothes you wear are part of marketing? I thought that. In fact, I know for sure that your attire and that of your employees, at least those who come into contact with your prospective customers, influence sales.

Ad specialties have been around as long as Adam, who probably displayed an apple calendar in his garden. But many businesses think of these doodads as something other than ultrapowerful marketing weapons. So I call your attention to them in this chapter, hoping you'll begin to use them to create some financial action—which you can do when you use them right.

I feel a pang of guilt when I mention this next marketing weapon. It's matchbooks. I surely do not want to contribute to the evil forces that make us smoke, having exorcised them from my own life about a quarter of a century ago. But I am compelled to tell you that matchbooks are part of direct marketing, and that they are the most effective part for many a company.

Finally, this chapter is about music. Music has this wondrous manner of accessing the unconscious mind of your prospects, and there are several opportunities for you to use music, whether or not you know it right now. So even though you may love music and walk around with your personal stereo headphones virtually attached to your ears, you may not realize that music is a canny marketing weapon that sounds as good, even better, than the jingle-jangle of your cash register—providing you use music as a true guerrilla.

We'll scrutinize all these marketing weapons in this chapter, and at the end of the chapter you may not decide to use all 16 of them, but you'll recognize that they are part of marketing. That realization will put you one leg up on your competition. And perhaps it will put you sixteen legs up. Naturally, that's what I hope.

Package

All companies have packages. And packages exert a powerful influence over human behavior.

Perhaps your package is your office. Maybe it's your sales representatives. It might be you yourself. Possibly your package is your store. It might even be your catalog. It may be the people who answer your telephone. And it may be the package in which your product is contained. The important point to remember is that, to a guerrilla marketer, your package is the primary physical manifestation of your business.

So don't delude yourself into thinking that if you don't have the type of package found on supermarket shelves you don't have a package. Virtually all businesses do have them, and most prospects unconsciously factor the package identity into their decision to buy—or not to buy.

What are the components of a package that would do a guerrilla proud? Glad you asked. First of all, it should clearly convey your identity. Second, it should have words, colors, and designs that inspire confidence. Third, it should have enough information so that a person can make an intelligent decision after studying it. And fourth, it should differentiate you from your competitors.

Your package should restate your theme, show your logo, and contain other materials to capitalize on your other marketing investments. You want people to see your package, then remember all of your other marketing.

When designing your package, keep in mind the medium you will be using to promote it. If, for instance, you plan on using television, be sure your package is photogenic. If people will see your package up close, pay attention to the details they will notice.

In all cases, regardless of type of package, remember that it is one of the most important components of marketing because of its ability to trigger an impulse sale. Prospects may have read all of your marketing materials and still be undecided about purchasing. That's when your package can tilt the scales in your favor.

Savvy marketers realize the importance of testing packages before committing to them. Many believe the package is the single most important selling tool they've got. Be sure your name is easy to read, your package is directed to your target audience, your package will be accepted (and loved) by your distributors, and your package clearly, but subtly, says "Buy me; try me; take me home; you'll be happy you did!" Above all, be sure your package looks like what it really is. Everyone has a package. Now that you know you do, too, put as much thought into it as into your other marketing weapons. And keep it consistent with your other marketing.

Business Cards

In the days before guerrilla marketers, business cards contained name, company, address, and phone number. Today, smart marketers are discovering that business cards can also contain the company theme and logo, then state its prime benefits.

Many cards use embossing, full color, or artwork if they wish to convey an identity those items might help.

These days, you can employ fold-over business cards; the front has the old-fashioned information, and the rest is like a minibrochure. People appreciate having complete information right on one small item along with the convenience of a business card.

Like many guerrillas, I employ several business cards. One is for my imported salmon business only. Another is solid brass for special occasions. One more is a color photo of me for use when my smiling face might be of help. Still another is a traditional kind with brown ink on tan card stock.

Business cards are only reminders—if your imagination limits you to that usage. But they also can be powerful selling tools, marketing vehicles that set you apart from your competition. Don't worry about the cost if one business card can net you a tidy profit. On the other hand, you might not even need a business card if none are used in your industry or if you won't have chances to distribute yours.

Stay with the standard business card size so that yours fits into a card storage file, wallet, or Rolodex. Use a typeface that is clear and easy to read—even by a person with bad eyesight. Be sure to include your area code (many bozos don't), your zip code, and your Fax number if you have one. Many guerrillas not only have one, but utilize it as still another marketing weapon.

Although you can have the printer design your card for free, be prepared to invest in a good art director if your cards will be used at trade shows, in mailings, or more than ordinarily. The feel of a good paper stock or the raised lettering of your copy can turn a prospect into a customer.

The prime points to remember in creating a business card are:

1. The business card is a marketing opportunity; use it.
2. Be unique without calling attention to your cleverness.
3. Give more information than the usual name, address, phone number.
4. Invest in a great-looking card if many prospects will see it.
5. Don't be skimpy when passing out your card. Be generous.

One very successful entrepreneur told me that his business card, really a minibrochure, was his single most important marketing tool. I can think of few vehicles so low in price that are seen by such a high ratio of honest prospects. And don't forget—when you hand out your business card, smile!

Stationery

Stationery means beans if you don't use it to communicate with large numbers of outside entities such as customers, suppliers, and prospects.

But stationery carries a potent message about your identity. So if you do use it with any of those entities, or others you may identify, it makes sense to invest talent and money in the design and production of stationery that will carry forth the banner you wave before your prospects.

Recognize that if you market according to traditional channels, only a tiny percentage of your prospects see your stationery. But perhaps your primary marketing vehicle is personal letters. Or maybe it is direct mailings. In either of those cases, your stationery is to you as Budweiser's TV commercials are to them: crucial.

Unless many important prospects will see your stationery, save money on the creation of it. Get the professional designer available at most printers to help you select a design, paper stock, a typeface, a color, the absence of color, formats, and the rest of the stationery components.

But you are plumb nuts to save money if the majority of your marketing funds will be invested in vehicles that make use of the stationery.

If that's the case, hire a first-rate graphics designer (check his or her portfolio first). Invest heavily in the paper stock you use so that it conveys a message that says you stand for higher quality and have higher standards than most organizations.

Consider using several colors. Think of the multiple uses to which you can put the stationery design other than letters and envelopes: notes, invoices, receipts, questionnaires, business cards, purchase orders, and a chunk of others, depending upon your business.

Many people will have their very first contact with you

via your stationery. Your envelope will begin to establish your identity. The logo, typeface, color, even the address, will reinforce the feelings. By the time the person opens the envelope, it has stated eloquently and silently that yours is a boring company, an exciting company, an innovative company, an old-fashioned company, a fifth-rate company —or something.

What you say in your letter will carry substantial weight. But don't overlook the unconscious influence exerted by your stationery. Plan on using the original design at least ten years.

The idea is not to save money on design but to get it right the first time and have it "feel" like your other marketing.

Order Form/Invoice

First, I want to be clear that an order form or invoice should clearly show the right numbers: date, price, and tax; plus the right words: customer name, product or service name, and your address. Other numbers and words usually appear on order forms and invoices to help clarify the minutiae of business.

But to a guerrilla, your communicating with the customer shouldn't end there. Once those matters are well in hand, with clarity being your byword, you can transform your order forms and invoices from bland business forms into powerful marketing weapons.

1. Always show your logo, big and bold, to implant this consummated sale in the mind of the customer.
2. Say something nice, like "Thank you" or "We appreciate your business" or anything that makes your impersonal relationship a bit more personal.
3. Consider your order form or invoice also to be an advertising opportunity. Say and show things on the forms to make customers feel better about you.
4. Pay close attention to all the wording on the form. Are requests stated politely? Are warmth and friendliness strived for? Does your wording seem different than the wording on other business forms your customer encounters?
5. Look into making your order form or invoice a brochure. Use it as the cover of a four-page brochure. Page 2 can be an ad. Page 3 can be a full "menu" listing all products and services you offer. Page 4 can be where you ask for the order and make it easy to place the order by means of a coupon, phone number, willingness to deliver, or even by asking the customer flat out to please come back.

Examine the paper stock, size, and color of your forms. Are they convenient for customers? Are they marketing for you? Can you print something on them (calendars/metric conversion charts/state capitals/local map/things of interest to your customers)?

The idea is to make the order form or invoice more than merely a boring business form. This is easy to do. Is it possible to make people happy that they owe you money? If you state ultrapositively what they received for their money, it is possible. A fund-raising company that took 50 percent as their profit used to send invoices reading: FOR FUND-RAISING SERVICES . . . $1,000. Then they changed to: CONGRATULATIONS! YOUR SCHOOL RAISED $2,000 SO $1,000 IS EXACTLY WHAT YOU OWE US. No wonder collection speed zoomed.

Now, I hope you transform your business forms—invoices, order forms, receipts, and the rest—into serious money-makers.

Inserts

When you read this, inserts will still be one of the better kept secrets in marketing. Five years from now, inserts will be far more common, and probably far less effective because of their abundance.

Inserts enable marketers to reach specific zip codes. That gives marketers far more accuracy than standard newspaper ads. What are inserts in the first place? They're those thin, colorful advertising supplements that are inserted right into the newspaper while it's folded. Inserts may not reach every family in a zip code this way, but there is one more way. If a family doesn't subscribe to a newspaper that carries the inserts, the inserts are mailed to them.

So no matter what happens, an insert is going to every address in the zip code. One of the greater advantages of inserts is the space they give you to market your goods or services. Usually, you have four or more full pages all to yourself. Not only that, but you have them to yourself in black, white and one or more colors. So you can say everything you've got to say, show a whole lot of what you've got to show.

What happens when an insert reaches an address? One of three things happens:

1. The insert promptly gets tossed in the garbage.
2. The insert gets read with the newspaper or the mail.
3. The insert gets saved, read carefully, and possibly carried to the place running the insert.

Right now, in my neck of the planet, the cost is $45 for every one thousand homes to which the insert is delivered. Add the cost of the insert—which can be high, if you want it to look like a magazine, or low, if you want it to look like a newspaper insert.

Inserts work best if you make a specific price offer and if that offer is of a limited-time nature. Businesses that have run inserts report that they last about thirty days, and sometimes even longer. But I suggest you time-limit yours to thirty days.

I also suggest that you pull out all the stops and tell all the good things about your place of business. Then make a dynamite offer designed to deliver a profit, but more important, to get people into your store for the first time.

Put those people onto your customer mailing list. If they respond to your insert, bet they'll respond to your post-card, too. Coupons work well in inserts. Experiment with zip codes and offers. Try various colors and insert lengths. Then stick with your winners. But I have a feeling you'll know that without this prodding from me.

Contests and Sweepstakes

There are five main reasons to have contests and sweepstakes:

1. To have people try your product or service
2. To make people aware of your product or service
3. To show people how to get to where you sell
4. To get names for your mailing list
5. To gain free publicity

Whichever your reason, understand that contests and sweepstakes are on the upswing because they succeed in the five purposes listed above. All five are noble goals for guerrillas, for they create momentum in the transformation of people from mere humans to paying customers.

In order to have a successful contest or sweepstakes, it is necessary to offer valuable prizes. The more prizes, the better. The better the prizes, the more people will enter.

A valuable guerrilla truth is that you often can obtain the prizes either for free or for a ridiculously low price. You accomplish this by making arrangements with local merchants or cooperative national marketers.

A travel agency, for instance, will probably be able to provide you with a good, but reduced-price, week in Hawaii, including airfare, accommodations, meals, and a car. The cost will be either nonexistent or laughably low—if you give a sufficient plug to the travel agency. That's fair.

Once you've lined up your prizes, you'll have to aggressively put out the word so as to attract the maximum number of entrants. Do this with newspaper ads, direct mailings, inserts, signs, tie-ins with others, circulars, and radio commercials. That's just a sampling of the ways available to publicize your contest.

If the prizes are attractive enough, perhaps your local

newspaper will write up the contest as a story. After all, they're interested in news. And if you're about to allow a local person to win a valuable prize and you're a local merchant—that's news in a local newspaper.

Be sure you also gain publicity after the winners have won their treasures—or holidays. Newspapers will usually be glad to do a story on the contest, prizes, and winners. Naturally, the star of the story will be your business. But only you will know if you're really a star, if the whole shebang resulted in a profit for you. But even if not, the new names on your mailing list can pay off later.

And a whole lot of people will no longer consider your company to be a stranger to them. My recommendation is to write to people within thirty days after they've entered your contest, while your name is still fresh in their minds.

Roadside Stands

If you live near an agricultural area, you've probably seen roadside stands offering fresh produce for sale. If you live near a tourist area, you've most likely noticed souvenirs sold from roadside stands. And if you reside in a hot-weather area, chances are you've seen cider, lemonade, or some other cooling beverage hawked from a roadside stand.

The truth is, however, that almost anything can be sold from a roadside stand. And you don't even have to invest in the stand or spend any time manning (or womanning) it—you might arrange a fusion marketing effort, where you supply the goods and give the roadside stand vendor a fair share of the take. After all, each stand is a new location for you.

Roadside stands are portable, flexible, inexpensive, appreciated by many bored and thirsty motorists, and just the ticket for areas that have a high concentration of traffic—either vehicular or pedestrian. Naturally, you've got to check with the local authorities to be sure you break no laws or infringe upon no other businesses. You should also be certain that there is adequate room for motorists to park in while they patronize your roadside stand. Shade is a plus as well.

You can arrange for a cooperative venture with the owner of an existing roadside stand or you can purchase and run one yourself. You can operate from your own location or you can set up in a highly traveled location. You can have a single roadside stand or you can have a string of them.

Signs will help your cause immeasurably. They should be on both sides of your stand. The optimum would be to have one three miles away, a second one mile away, a third five hundred feet away, and a fourth right at the stand. That's a total of seven signs. But if you letter them clearly, realizing that the readers might be zooming by at fifty-five miles per hour, they can attract a horde of welcome business.

In many parts of the United States, roadside stands are quite commonplace. But in the majority of the nation, where they are rare, roadside stands can be marketing brilliance. They are the very essence of convenience; they reach people who may be right in the market for what you are selling; they enable transactions to be conducted speedily and simply.

Naturally, the decor of your stand will influence sales, as will the signs you have right there at the stand and on each side of it. Guerrillas see to it that their stands are works of marketing art and that their signs are enticing and informative. If you've always wanted multiple locations, roadside stands are a great way to benefit from them without the attendant high cost of expansion. And consider their use at fairs, malls, and hypermarkets. Roadside stands can be used at many places other than sides of roads.

Gift Baskets

If you're like most people, you associate gift baskets with department stores and perhaps gift stores. If you're a guerrilla marketer, you associate gift baskets with bookstores, car dealers, computer consultants, clothing stores, and your own business.

The underlying concept behind gift baskets is the grouping of several items in one package—primarily to be given as a gift.

There are two major benefits to gift baskets:

1. Your customers appreciate the thought you've put behind the overall package.
2. Your CPA appreciates the increased cash flow.

Everyone wins with gift baskets—especially during Christmastime, when everyone is searching for new and unusual gift ideas, but throughout the year as well.

A bookstore chain decided to explore the idea of gift baskets. Instead of selling one cookbook at a time, they packaged five cookbooks, displayed them in a wicker basket covered with cellophane, and put a bright red bow around them. Customers ended up buying five books instead of one. And they were grateful for the suggestions of the other four.

Car dealers have put together gift baskets of accessories, including car stereos, service certificates, and detailing certificates. A car dealer with a gift basket? They sure worked for those dealers who have tried them.

Use your imagination to combine products and/or services that you offer. Package them together. Maybe even put them into a wicker gift basket. Then let your audience know that you now offer these gift baskets.

Display them. Offer them in direct mailings—especially to customers. Mention them in ads. You'll be happily surprised at how many people appreciate their availability.

Don't limit yourself to retail thinking. It's easy for a retailer to come up with a gift basket. It's tougher for a consultant. But if that consultant offers a gift basket that includes consultation time, a book or two, a videotape, and an audiotape, suddenly that consultant has a gift basket that may be purchased by the end user or given as a gift.

Naturally, if you don't have a window in which to display your gift basket, try to tie in with a company that does have a window. Offer your gift basket to catalog companies. They're always on the lookout for unique offerings. A gift basket might be just the ticket for them, for their customers, and for you. Wouldn't you like a gift basket as a present?

Audiovisual Aids

Facts presented to the ear and eye are 68 percent more effective than facts presented to the ear alone. That's because people absorb the vast majority of information in their lives visually. As a guerrilla, this indicates that you should show whatever you are talking about.

You can accomplish this with comprehensive use of audiovisual aids. These marketing devices take on many forms: signs, flip charts, slide shows, videotapes, brochures, posters, photographs, you name it.

Audiovisual aids prove of enormous benefit in several areas. First, they can tell your entire story to prospects, serving as "silent salespeople." Second, they can help your salespeople demonstrate points visually. Third, they can clarify many otherwise complex sales points you wish to make. And fourth, they are attention-getting and far more appealing than mere words.

Naturally, the best audiovisual aids are a combination of words and pictures. The pictures can be photos, illustrations, or diagrams. Whichever they are, they will make your points easier to remember and understand.

There are many cases when nonproductive salespeople became ultraproductive simply because they were furnished with audiovisual sales aids—usually with the salesperson supplying the live audio presentation and using the charts, graphs, or electronic visual aids as enhancement.

Audiovisual aids can be remarkably inexpensive to produce. They allow you to show your product or service in use; they can show before and after visuals; they can vividly demonstrate your sales points. It is the combination of audio and visual appeals that has helped make TV such a powerful marketing medium. And yet, you need not go beyond simple line drawings or diagrams to make verbal points visually.

If you randomly selected one hundred people and offered to give them directions to a specific location, about fifty would want the directions written out and about fifty would want a map. It is for that latter 50 percent of your prospects that audiovisual aids work so well—in penetrating deep into the mind, in making your story clear, and in helping your story be remembered.

A salesperson who is not supplied with audiovisual aids—in the form of a script, a fact sheet, and visual enhancement of both—is being robbed of his or her potential effectiveness. A guerrilla marketer will always make these aids available to a sales force and will ask members of the sales force if any further audiovisual aids will help them in their cause, then create the types salespeople feel will make them better at their job. No question about it: Show-and-tell is a shortcut to show-and-sell.

Audiotapes and Videotapes

Over 94 percent of Americans have access to audiocassette players in their homes or cars; over 70 percent have video-cassette players. Both numbers are growing. And so are the numbers of guerrilla marketers who have come to learn that these machines represent superb marketing opportunities.

Rather than employing radio, television, direct mail, or the usual marketing weapons, they opt for the unusual. They give their hot prospects audiotapes or videotapes selling their services.

The cost to produce a first-class audiotape can be under $500 and up to $5,000. The cost to produce a first-class videotape can run from $5,000 to $50,000. Both require voice talent; both are improved with the use of music. But only the videotape lets you demonstrate your product. And the ability to demonstrate is one of the greatest advantages of advertising on television.

You should consider using an audiotape if you are certain that your prospects will take the time to listen to it. This is best assured if they have a car with a cassette player, as so many businesspeople do these days.

Use their time with the audiocassette to motivate them to buy what you are selling, using a combination of voices, music, and sound effects. A single voice heard for a long period is boring. I suggest anywhere from five minutes to sixty minutes as proper for a sales-oriented audiocassette.

If you plan to market with a videocassette, the times are considerably shorter: seven to twelve minutes seems optimum for those trying and loving this weapon.

Be sure your cassettes are professionally produced or they'll lose as many sales for you as they'll gain. Saving money on production of these cassettes is a false economy.

Find people who wish to hear your cassettes rather than mailing them helter-skelter. You can locate these people with ads featuring the main benefits of dealing with your company, then offering a free audio- or videocassette.

By giving them away, you increase the chance of multiple viewings and pass-along viewership. Only serious prospects will send away for the cassettes and take the time to give them the attention they deserve. Of course, curiosity-seekers who love freebies will also request them.

Think of audio- and videocassettes as high-tech marketing. Meaning: Their prime purpose is to gain orders for you. Businesses of all types are learning that there are rich profits to be earned in the Age of the Electronic Brochure.

Marketing on Phone Hold

These days, when you call a business, there's a very good chance that your phone call will be put on hold. Frequently, you're kept waiting so long that the situation can accurately be called "permahold."

Some companies, rather than keep you waiting in silence, will connect the phone to a radio station so that you can listen to music, bad or good, along with commercials. Occasionally, a commercial will herald the glories of a company that competes with the company you are calling.

What to do? Market to the people who are on hold. That's what to do. When this happens, the caller is automatically connected to a sound track that plays music befitting your identity while listening to messages of interest to them: special offers available from you, benefits of dealing with you, facts that will appeal to the caller. When this happens, rather than resent you, callers will honestly appreciate the information you are putting forth.

I have one client with marketing-on-hold messages that are so intriguing that callers who get through to the person they are calling actually ask to be put on hold!

You can learn a lot more about the high effectiveness of this advanced marketing technique, along with its surprisingly low cost, if you contact a company specializing in this type of marketing.

One such company, Information-on-Hold, may be reached by calling 408-980-8282. Ask them for their free brochure. In it, you'll learn how the technology works, why it is effective, and how simple it is to add this weapon to your arsenal. This company and others like it, such as Muzak, will select the appropriate music for you, create the scripts you'll need, and produce the finished sound tracks. The cost will be considerably less than you may expect. And the finished product will be impressive and professional.

You can keep your marketing-on-hold cost even lower if you do the job yourself: select your own music, write your own scripts, voice your own message.

This entire concept is the very essence of guerrilla marketing: it talks directly to customers and prospects; it turns a potentially negative situation into a positive one; it provides a service to callers, many of whom will purchase goods and/or services that they may not have known you offered. And it takes more imagination than money to do it.

Many potential customers hang up rather than wait in silence or listen to a radio station. Marketing-on-phone-hold is a way of transforming them from disgruntled callers into satisfied and enlightened customers.

Decor

Regardless of what you say in your marketing materials, people will make judgments about your business based in great part on the decor of your physical plant, be it store or office.

This is one of those factors, not often associated with marketing, that exerts a powerful influence on the unconscious mind of your prospects and customers.

It is crucial that your decor accurately reflect the identity you communicate with your marketing. When it does, people feel a sense of trust that you portrayed yourself honestly. If yours is an avant-garde business, the decor should be avant-garde in every way. If yours is a homey, old-fashioned identity, the decor can't be avant-garde or the prospects will be confused.

Your decor should influence people to trust you. It should not necessarily win design awards. In fact, decor that is too slick might dampen the effects of a marketing strategy based on low prices.

Your interior decorator should read your marketing strategy so that every item of decor mirrors that strategy. I suppose it is a shame that people make purchase (or no-purchase) decisions based on your furniture, wallpaper, lighting fixtures, wall hangings, carpeting, window treatments, and color schemes. But they do. And as a practicing guerrilla, you should be delighted at the opportunity to add to the marketing momentum you have generated with your other marketing weaponry.

Decor to a business is like attire to a sales representative. The prospects must first buy the business before they'll buy the products or services sold by the business. They'll buy it if your decor shows pride in your business, quality throughout, cleanliness, and an absence of shabbiness.

Be careful you don't overdecorate, spending so lavishly

on your store or office that your prospects sense they will be supporting your fancy overhead when they pay for what you sell. On the other hand, if an elegant chandelier or coffee table will further convince your prospects of your quality or success, invest in the best. It's worth it.

People will not only judge your company by your decor, but they will place great importance upon this judgment because they assume your decor better reflects your company than your marketing. After all, marketing is supposed to influence people; decor isn't. But it does. And guerrillas know it, so they can take full advantage of this potent marketing weapon. I hope you do, too, with decor selected for its ability to carry forth your identity, decor that you recognize as a marketing opportunity.

ATTIRE

In increasing numbers, people are coming to realize that attire influences human behavior. While navy blue signifies authority, brown shows a lack of sophistication. While black shows almost too much power, red calls a great deal of attention to the wearer. Each color puts forth its own message.

People in the most chic and up-to-date styles draw interest away from their primary topic, unless that topic is fashion.

When in a dilemma about how dressy you should be, always tend to be more formal than more informal. It's much easier to dress down a bit than dress up a bit.

Although this should go without saying, I've seen too many instances when, by its being unsaid, sales were lost. Be sure clothes are neat, shoes are shined, hair is in place, hands and face are clean. There's little that can nip a sale in the bud as effectively as an employee in messy or dirty garb.

Although it is good for employees to feel happy and free, your company is better off if those employees visible to your prospects and customers follow a dress code that calls at least for cleanliness and an absence of inappropriate attire. Hair length can vary as long as it does not call attention to itself and away from the product or service for sale. Some guerrillas in a retail environment ask that all their employees wear company shirts—white oxford button-downs with the company's logo and name in color. This makes the employees visible to customers. On a crowded sales floor, this uniformity in attire clearly identifies the workers from the shoppers. Says one guerrilla of this, "We don't want customers to wonder about anything in our stores."

Other guerrillas have discovered that by requesting their male employees to wear dark suits and ties, their female employees to wear dark suits or dresses plus hose and heels, sales soared even though prices were raised.

The dignity and good taste of some attire is unconsciously transferred to the product or service. Same for the nonchalance and questionable taste of other attire.

Guerrillas realize that they must sell themselves before they can sell the product or service. The proper attire helps them make this sale. They also know for a fact that many people will judge their business by the employee with the tackiest taste in clothes.

For these reasons, business owners should think carefully about instituting a dress code. If it can honestly improve profits, it is an inexpensive and very guerrillalike way of marketing. After all, not every guerrilla is clad in camouflage-hued fatigues.

Ad Specialties and Gifts

One of the most delightful, versatile, rewarding, winning, cost-effective, proven, and disarming of all the marketing weapons is free gifts, also known as advertising specialties.

To get an idea of how wide a selection there is in this field, look in your yellow pages under "Advertising Specialties," call the company with the best ad, and check the catalog of gifts offered by that company. Chances are, the catalog will run several thousand pages, each one providing you a host of options you can use to lure customers into your business or into sending or calling for more information about your business.

As one with the soul and spirit of a guerrilla, you already know the humongous power of bribes to elicit a response. Well, these gifts and ad specialties are the bribes to which I refer. If you wish to get a free catalog of the best gifts/ bribes I've ever seen—all with a high perceived value and a ridiculously low price, ask for the free catalog from the people at Schmidt-Cannon, 818-961-9871. They offer gifts for virtually any target market.

Strong recommendation: Check out the catalog and offer some of the gifts to get people into your place of business, to request more data, or even to make a purchase. Regardless of their income group, people love free gifts. Have I ever seen an exception to this? Never. And I've been looking.

In the past, the hottest ad specialties were calendars and ballpoint pens. These days, the hot ones seem to be scratch pads (everyone uses them, and your name, logo, theme, and address appear before prospects almost daily); electronic gizmos such as clock pens, desk clocks, and microcalculators; and even matches.

These days you also see many ad specialties at work in the form of imprinted T-shirts, baseball caps, belt buckles, lighters, license-plate frames, shopping bags, playing cards, key chains, and zillions more. Although gifts won't do the marketing job all by themselves, they should be seriously considered as part of your guerrilla marketing arsenal. Still, order the minimum quantity to start.

Free gifts create a sense of unconscious obligation to purchase on the part of the consumer, but that's not why you should use them. I predict you'll love the ability of advertising specialties to generate leads, goodwill, lasting value, usefulness to promote special events, and eventual profits for your company.

Matchbooks

At first glance, matchbooks hardly seem to be an effective marketing weapon. But consider the case of International Correspondence Schools (ICS). They've been using coupons printed inside matchbooks since 1881. And they receive about 300,000 responses annually from their matchbook marketing.

Merely advertising on matchbooks is much like advertising on billboards. It's nice for restaurants, possibly also for cigarettes. But it's hardly a way to build a business. You can count on it to remind people of your marketing theme and thrust, but that's about it. Unless you're a guerrilla.

Guerrillas use matchbooks as direct response weapons. They use the outside of the matchbook to herald their benefits, then use the inside to print a coupon that enables the matchbook user to send for more information—thereby landing that prospect smack dab on your mailing list.

Companies that print matchbooks also offer services in design and distribution. They can not only arrange for distribution where you request, but can also come up with several ideas that may not have entered your mind. And they can place your matchbooks in all the cigarette machines in a given locality. Each smoker who purchases a pack of cigarettes also receives a matchbook—plus your ad, offer, and coupon.

The cost of matchbook marketing is extremely low—especially if you use the books simply to urge prospects to request further data. They are not effective at closing sales. But you probably know that already.

It may be worth your time to contact one of the matchbook printers in your locality and meet with a sales rep. Learn what other types of companies have used this device. Find out the results they achieved.

Many companies have been employing matchbook marketing for decades. They sure wouldn't stay with the medium if it didn't obtain positive results for them. Find out what they say on their matchbooks. Pick the brain of the matchbook sales rep. The rep ought to be able to convince you that matchbooks are your ideal medium. If not, steer clear.

Don't commit to a matchbook campaign unless you have tested the copy, coupon, offer, and points of distribution first. Once you've come up with a winner, this method of marketing might be enough to light up your sales curve for years to come. ICS did it. Many other companies gain the majority of their leads via this little-known route.

Perhaps you can, too. As a guerrilla, you ought to at least check out the idea.

Music

Many guerrilla marketers have gained customers and profits because they were associated with a particular music. Some of these guerrillas invested heavily ($5,000–$250,000) in having an original music track created for them. Others invested minimally ($500–$2,000), using a nonname talent. And still others kept their costs down even more by using "library music"—a wide selection of good but nonexclusive music available at many recording studios. Another term for this is *rights-free* music.

In case you're wondering what use you may have for your own music, allow me to suggest several: as background music for radio or TV commercials, as the musical theme behind your marketing messages delivered while people who call your company are put on hold, as the music in your audiotape or videotape marketing efforts, and as music played at key presentations. Possibilities also include music used at a trade show booth, a sales meeting, a show for prospects or employees, and a company convention.

Music accesses the unconscious minds of your customers and prospects, helping to earn the important share of mind that comes before share of market. One radio expert claims that music adds 30 percent more power to your spoken words in this manner. Although many guerrillas use the same music track for years and years, knowing that its powers of subliminal persuasion improve with time and familiarity, others keep the same musical theme but vary the arrangements depending on the markets they are attempting to reach.

The music you select or have created should further your identity and be in keeping with your company personality. Always keep in mind the longevity factor: Don't use music that will become outdated. Stay with timeless music instead.

Music influences the way people think about your company, adds punch to your spoken words, establishes a mood. And the more your prospects hear your music, the better they will feel about it—and your company. Of course, this will happen on an unconscious level.

Music also serves to make your marketing theme more memorable, such as "The Valley of the Jolly Green Giant" or "This Bud's for You." Because of its power and flexibility, music is a potent weapon for any guerrilla marketing arsenal.

Don't expect it to do the whole selling job for you, only to enhance your current marketing. If you do invest a few thousand dollars in a music track, the amortized cost over a period of years makes it a wise investment. Almost any music can aid your message. But the very best music is that which is clearly associated with your company, instantly identifies you to your prospects and customers, and actually excites them about your business. Such is the power of music.

4
WEAPONS THAT BEGIN WITH ATTITUDES

The 12 weapons in this chapter have several things in common, one of the most important being that they don't cost you one cent. Twelve weapons and you don't pay a penny. It doesn't make sense *not* to use them.

These weapons are attitudes—mind-sets focused upon employing guerrilla marketing tactics consistently and throughout your organization.

Many companies have prospered to impressive degrees by utilizing several of these 12 free weapons.

You will have few opportunities in your business life to gain so much while investing so little. In the true spirit of guerrilla marketing, this requires that you or your designated guerrilla—the person who directs your marketing for you—invest time, energy, and imagination. Instilling attitudes that beget profitability begins with hiring the right people. Some of these attitudes will be direct reflections of your talent in hiring and training of others. Other attitudes rest squarely on your gumption.

When you complete this chapter, you will know exactly

how simple, yet rugged, the terrain is for a guerrilla. Marketing will move to the realm of psychology once again as you attempt to mold human behavior, yours and others.

It's not going to be easy to implant and maintain these attitudes. It's going to be no picnic maintaining them for the first six months or so. But once you see the results of embracing these attitudes, the job of fueling your marketing fires will become a great deal easier.

As with almost all marketing tactics, the launching of these efforts will demand the most of you. But succeeding in business demands no less; feel grateful for the chance to display your talents in these arenas. If you lack the talents, your designated guerrilla ought to be able to supply them handily.

Perhaps you cannot afford to employ some of the other weapons in this book. For example, videotape marketing may be beyond your reach at this time. But you cannot afford to ignore these 12 weapons. Weapons that begin with attitudes are the weapons of winners.

When the combatants square off in the Super Bowl, their sizes and shapes will vary little. But their attitudes will win the game—or lose it. In business, there are winners and losers, too. Very often, mere attitudes make all the difference.

As with all books crammed with advice, it is very easy for you to read and me to write of these attitudes. But to make them a part of the very essence of your company— that's where the guerrillas get separated from the wimps.

Depending on the nature of your business, some of these weapons will have no application for you. Others will make a major impact on your profits. Your phone demeanor will turn prospects on or off in a jiffy. It's up to you. This is one of the most powerful of the weapons, yet is actually an attitude that is yours for the asking—if you ask the right people and train them properly.

The neatness, and its opposite number, sloppiness, of your premises will cause prospects and customers to think about you. The kind of thoughts they think is up to you.

Who would think that something as commonplace as a smile could be a marketing weapon? A guerrilla would think so and realize that smiles aren't as commonplace as you imagine, especially in business encounters.

Speed is a more important weapon today than it was twenty years ago, when people placed less of a premium on their time. When you can, prove your customer devotion by acting rapidly. Customers will appreciate your quick response time.

Everyone knows that service is a weapon that begins with an attitude. It's one thing to be able to perform a service. It's another thing for customers to feel in their bones that you want to solve their problems, want to make their lives better, want to render service.

Not everyone knows that follow-up is a weapon that, when not employed, leads to failure and, when employed with savvy, leads to riches. I hope for your sake that you can employ this weapon with constancy and flair.

Contact time with the customer is a weapon not available to many businesses. If yours can use it, do what you must so your employees realize they should develop attitudes that treat this time as a marketing opportunity, a time for gentle suggestion and business bonding.

If you own a restaurant, you probably know that a mighty weapon is knowing how to say hello and good-bye. There are many wrong ways. There's only one right way. You'll read about it right up ahead. If you can imbue the right attitude about this weapon throughout your organization, your financial director will notice the difference.

You don't need me to tell you how free publicity will help you. But you probably do need me to let you know that publicity will not be spewing forth abundantly unless you have an abundance of publicity contacts—people working for the media; people with power, influence, and the ability to say "Print this" to a subordinate. Is it difficult to obtain these contacts? Of course it is. Now ask me if it's worth your time and trouble.

The tenth on this list of 12 weapons is an attitude that either you or your designated guerrilla must have. It's nice if your employees have it, too, but it doesn't mean diddly if *you* don't make sure it happens. This weapon is called brand-name awareness, and you already know its importance based on your own inclination to purchase brand names. It takes time and a committed leader to build this awareness, but over the long haul, you're sunk without it.

Enthusiasm is the attitude that moves many a prospect off the fence and onto the dotted line. The spark begins with you—every minute, every day, every year. It spreads to your management, then to employees, and finally to prospects, who become customers, who tell their friends because they're enthusiastic. A happy scenario. Just don't forget where the spark originated, boss.

Competitiveness is the twelfth and most important of the 12 attitude weapons. It is your responsibility. It is you who must learn about the 100 weapons available to you, then activate as many as feasible. If you have this attitude, the others will fall into place, neat and tidy. Do you lack this attitude? Then run, don't walk, to the person in or out of your firm who can best serve as your designated guerrilla. If you don't compete, you can't win.

PHONE DEMEANOR

The way your phone is answered and the way callers are treated exerts a powerful influence upon the profitability of your company.

Adherence to seven rules can transform a ringing telephone into a potent guerrilla marketing weapon:

1. Institute a brief but clear telephone training program. In it, instruct employees how to answer and not answer the phone, how to communicate effectively with callers, how to develop a friendly phone attitude, and how to convey any specific points you wish to cover to all callers. Do not let anyone who has not taken your training program answer the phone. The program can run as short as one hour and be summarized on a single page. Do it. It always pays off. And it doesn't cost much to initiate. Repeat it quarterly.

2. See to it that your phone is answered the same way each time to give callers the comfort of consistency. The answer should be friendly and mention the company name. More important, it should have a built-in warm smile.

3. Recognize that time is of increasing importance. So handle phone calls comprehensively, directly, and fast. Callers will appreciate the respect you have for their time.

4. If you wish to make outbound phone calls to create leads or sales, contact your telephone company and ask if they offer free seminars. Many do. And be sure to read about telemarketing scripts in Chapter 7.

5. If you do not have enough phone lines, rather than putting callers on hold or transferring them to a line with a radio station that just might be playing a commercial for one of your competitors, transfer them to

a background of beautiful music and a message about your company, including any special offers you have at the time. Get more data on this by calling Information-on-Hold at 408-980-8282 or Muzak at 800-858-1900.

6. Although you may not wish to give prices over the phone for reasons of your own, try to answer the caller's questions as clearly and sincerely as possible. If you must, quote price ranges rather than specific numbers. But the more specific you can be, the better.

7. Be polite regardless of the caller's attitude. Talk yourself into believing that customers and prospects are always right—even when they're wrong.

The telephone call is an opportunity for people to form first impressions, and for you to display professionalism and demonstrate that you've got the right attitudes. If you don't recognize that every phone call is a marketing opportunity, you're not a practicing guerrilla.

NEATNESS

You won't find neatness listed in any marketing textbooks or discussed in many marketing classes, yet the presence—or absence—of neatness exerts a powerful effect upon a person's decision to purchase. There is little question that neatness is a potent and inexpensive marketing weapon.

You'd be astonished if you knew how many people decide not to do business with a company that has displayed sloppiness on their premises, in their business practices, or with their marketing.

These people make the unconscious but natural assumption that if a company is sloppy in any way, that must show up in how they run their business. The same, happily, is true of neatness. If your prospects see it physically or sense it intellectually, they assume that you are a together company that doesn't make mistakes.

Neatness refers to your store, office, premises, delivery vehicles, sales reps, service people, telephone people, signs, and correspondence.

It is a simple matter to ascertain the neatness of these entities on a Monday morning. It is quite a different thing to maintain the neatness throughout the entire day and the entire week. Still, you can and will be judged at any time. And neatness or sloppiness will be part of that judgment. The people who run Disneyland know that very well and set the standards for neatness as a continuing marketing endeavor.

Rarely does a single thing influence a purchase decision. More often, it is a series of items that causes prospects to form opinions. Neatness, though far less heralded, less glamorous (and less expensive) than advertising, is one of those items. It is too important to be overlooked.

This realization should be imparted to every person in your employ. It is the job of each of them to maintain neatness at all times and in all phases of your business.

Although it is true that some people can overlook a clump of mud in your front doorway or a layer of scum on your countertop, many others cannot. And even if you have created genius-level marketing to attract these people, you probably haven't got a prayer of selling them. They have seen that your business is messy.

If the environment is appealing, the items sold will be more appealing. Nobody wants to purchase dusty merchandise or see dirt in an office. If you can't afford janitorial services, assign the neatness to your staff—or yourself.

Guerrillas think of their businesses as their homes and their prospects as their guests. You wouldn't invite guests to a cluttered home. Don't expect them to buy from a business that looks unappealing. You wouldn't, would you?

SMILES

You can pore over all the marketing tomes in the world, then attend all the classes and seminars. Still, you'll probably never hear a marketing authority, unless you hear me, say that one of the most important factors in marketing is a simple smile. Yet that's the guerrilla truth.

A smile forms a human bond, far more powerful than a mere business bond. A smile shows you consider the person a human being rather than a nameless consumer or member of a demographic group. It proves you have singled the person out as special. It says you are personally interested.

Best of all, it makes the person feel good, feel that you are a friend. And people just love to buy from friends.

Most businesspeople are just in too much of a hurry to smile honestly at their prospects and customers. They take business too seriously. Smiles do wonders at breaking down barriers, establishing relationships, imparting warmth, and proving humanity.

Ask yourself: How many times did a business owner smile at me during the past month? Once? Twice? Probably less. How would it make you feel if a business owner did smile at you? It would make you feel wonderful. No wonder you would be likely to regularly patronize the business.

Smiles are part of the spirit of guerrilla marketing because they don't cost one cent. Yes, they take time, and they ask for energy on your part. They also require sincerity. And they come to vibrant life if you look the person in the eye while you are smiling. That is relatively deep human contact in the context of business.

But smiles also work on the telephone because people can actually "hear" the smile. So eye contact helps, but is not always absolutely necessary. A smile is proof that you like the person, that you appreciate the person's business, that the person makes you happy. A sour expression accomplishes the opposite. I'll bet this doesn't surprise you.

Successful business management requires attention not only on the broad scene, but also on the tiny details. A smile is one of those details. Once you understand the importance of a smile, be sure you impart your understanding to all employees who will deal with the public. Happy companies are pleasant to do business with. Smiles clearly state to the unconscious mind that yours is a happy company and make dealing with your company an enjoyable experience.

Smiles appear to be minor and tiny in the scope of things. But they're far more important than they appear. That's why there are so many smiling guerrillas. And that's why they have so many repeat and referral customers.

SPEED

According to the most recent studies of our current society, the most precious asset a person possesses is time.

People's time is required at work, at home, with the family, attending to errands, doing many things that do not fall under the headings of relaxation or recreation. For this reason, they revere their free time. And as a guerrilla marketer, so should you. I also heartily suggest that you read *The Ninety-Minute Hour*—a book I wrote (and E. P. Dutton published in 1990) about the very topic on this page. Don't believe the big lie that time is money. Utter nonsense! Time is far more valuable than money.

People expect speed in their business dealings now more than ever. They want their phone call to be handled fast. They want to be waited on in a hurry. They want their orders processed with lightning speed. They want their complaints handled without delay. They are busy people with tons of details to attend to; they don't want to be kept waiting by you. Guerrillas organize their businesses so as to offer this speed. They are aware of the public impatience with waiting, so they don't make their customers wait. And they gain the customers of businesses that don't respect the time of their customers.

Speed not only holds on to existing customers, it also attracts prospective customers. And the lack of speed loses customers just as the lack of service does. In fact, speed is considered a component of service.

Just look around at all the Minute Auto Lube and Twenty-Minute Haircuts and Jiffy Auto Tuning and One-Hour Photo Lab franchises and you can understand what I mean.

I mean handle your prospects' and customers' requests without making them wait more than is absolutely necessary. Listen to them, then act on what they say. Don't get bogged down by the tradition of making them wait a week. Make them wait one hour, if that. Knock yourself out showing how much you respect their time.

Convey your reverence of their time in your ads, in your brochures, in your signs. A medical clinic advertises: "If you aren't seen by a professional within twenty minutes, your office visit is free." No wonder the clinic is so successful. Do you think they made up that theme line out of thin air? Nope. It was the result of customer research, which showed that customers resent waiting more than anything else. Almost everyone has a horror story about waiting a millennium to see the doctor.

The same may be true of your customers. There are many areas in which you can demonstrate your speed, your realization of the importance of your customers' time. Do all you can to prove that you sincerely care about that time and that you are doing all in your power to act with speed.

SERVICE

Your overriding feelings in business should be: customer love, customer satisfaction, and customer convenience. Make it as easy as possible to buy what you are selling. That means taking phone orders, accepting as many credit cards as possible, having a toll-free number, and arranging your days and hours around the lives of your customers.

This is crucial because service is the third most important factor influencing a purchase decision, ranking right after confidence and quality.

Although you may memorize the words on these pages, it is equally important that every employee who deals with your public feels the same sense of *wanting* to provide superb service. It's the wanting that makes the big difference.

Service is an ongoing function, starting with a customer's first contact with you, making itself apparent during the time of the sale, and continuing on well after delivery of your offering. Follow-up service equals repeat and referral sales—the best kind. Customers may have never heard of the concept of a customer-oriented business, but you can be sure that they know when a business is not.

Service should always be speedy, courteous, and better than the customer dreamed it would be. Give more than they expect and you've made a friend for life. Never ignore or argue with a customer.

Service means solving your customers' problems, attending to their needs, making their lives better because they bought what you are selling. You can perform this kind of service if you remember the Guerrilla's Golden Rule: ALWAYS TRY TO THINK LIKE YOUR CUSTOMER.

Companies excelling in service have seven things in common:

1. They set amazingly high standards of performance.
2. They are obsessed with knowing what the customer wants.

3. They know that customer expectations must be understood and managed before they can be met and exceeded.
4. They design their products and services to maximize customer satisfaction.
5. They knock themselves silly trying to be an easy company with which to do business and it clearly shows.
6. They know the money they invest in customer service will pay off in satisfaction for customers, profits for them.
7. They repeat and repeat again that customer service is the responsibility of everyone in the organization.

Customer service is really common sense. Walk a few miles in your customers' shoes and you'll soon know what turns them on—and off. Remember that they buy to fulfill expectations. And these days, they expect excellent service.

FOLLOW-UP

The difference between a guerrilla marketer and a non-guerrilla marketer is that the nonguerrilla thinks that the marketing is over when the sale has been made.

The guerrilla, realizing the immense potential value of each customer, begins the all-out marketing attack *when* the sale is made. The guerrilla knows that each customer is a potential repeat customer and a potential referral source leading to other customers.

So the follow-up begins with a thank-you note or card within one week of the purchase. When's the last time a business thanked you for being a customer?

The follow-up continues on a regular basis, using one or more of many follow-up opportunities. The number of these is as limitless as your imagination. Here's a year's worth:

1. A preferred-customer show
2. A birthday card
3. A private sale
4. A newsletter
5. A letter with a fact of interest plus a special offer
6. A postcard mailing program
7. A telemarketing offer
8. A Christmas card
9. A contest or sweepstakes
10. The anniversary of when your customer became your customer
11. A research questionnaire
12. An audio brochure and customer-only offering

Stay in touch with your customers, because if you don't, someone else will. Eighty percent of business that is lost is lost due to apathy after the sale. Built-in follow-up, set up as an automatic procedure by your company, is a safeguard against apathy. It requires time, energy, and imagination—as does all guerrilla marketing. But it does not require a lot of money.

Recognize that a customer representing a $200 profit to you can mean a $200 profit without follow-up. Or that same customer can mean a $60,000 profit with follow-up. The arithmetic works like this:

- Follow-up transforms the $200 profit into a $600 yearly profit per customer (with two repeat sales).
- Follow-up results in four referrals, each representing $600, a total of $2,400 per year. $2,400 plus $600 equals $3,000.
- Even if you earn no more referrals after the first year, $3,000 times a normal twenty-year relationship with customers means at least a $60,000 profit per customer —if you do follow-up. If you don't, you miss out on $59,800.

CONTACT TIME WITH THE CUSTOMER

In some businesses, the customers order by mail. In others, they call an 800 number and talk to a professional operator. In many, they walk in, make their purchase, pay, and walk out. Owners of these businesses are denied a valuable marketing opportunity that is reserved for those who have the luxury of time with their customers.

This time can be used to strengthen the human bond, the business bond, the spiritual bond. It can be used to learn what the customer wants and needs so that you can be of better service. The customer will sense your caring attitude.

Because of the buyer-seller relationship between you, the time you are together is time you can use to make your customer aware of your other offerings and the benefits of purchasing them. This should not be approached in a pressured manner, but in an honest, businesslike way.

If the customer bought a product, offer a companion product or service. If the customer bought a service, offer a companion service or product.

Perhaps you can learn from your customer of other people who ought to be your customers. Letters to them could prove fruitful, especially if you can mention names. Get permission from your customer to use his or her name in such letters.

The underlying idea of contact time with customers as a marketing weapon is the foundation of high-quality small business: you do everything you can to provide your customer maximum satisfaction, consistently improving your service or products or both. With this as your goal, you will convince customers of your dedication to excellence whenever they spend time with you.

This will motivate them to want to do business with you . . . to want to refer business to you . . . to want your business to succeed.

If you understand this, it will not only improve the quality of your business but it will help your business market itself during times that are unrecognized as marketing opportunities by nonguerrillas (a term I hope describes your competition).

Opportunities for contact time with your customer arise when the customer is buying the product or receiving the service you offer, when the customer is shopping, when the customer comes in for repairs, updating, even to register a complaint! All of these are opportunities for you to render superb service in the matter that concerns the customer—and to market your other offerings. A national chain of styling salons increased profits 29 percent by marketing products while providing services. You might even consider using valuable customer contact time to market the goods or services of others—as long as the customer benefits.

HOW YOU SAY HELLO AND GOOD-BYE

Glamorous marketing devices such as magazine ads, TV commercials, informative brochures, and gorgeous offices may cost a lot and earn a lot of profits for you.

You can also earn healthy profits with zero investment if you know how to say hello and good-bye to customers, prospects, and even total strangers. Smile, look the person directly in the eyes, and mention the person's name.

If you're saying hello or good-bye by phone, do all but the eye contact part. People love being treated like human beings with minds and feelings. Among their favorite things is the sound of their own name. If you don't know it when you say hello, learn it, then by all means use it when you say good-bye.

Ask yourself how many businesspeople you dealt with last month smiled, looked you in the eye, and said your name when they said hello or good-bye. If you're like most of us, the answer is between one and zero. So you can be sure you will stand out if you bring the practice to life.

It is human nature that people enjoy doing business with people they like. They will like you more if you smile, look them directly in the eye, and mention their name. It will make them feel special. It will prove to their unconscious mind that you will always treat them specially.

So they'll come back to do more business. They'll feel comfortable recommending your company to a friend or associate.

It's pretty easy to sit there and read about how to say hello and good-bye. But it is a tough task to make certain that all of your employees understand the wisdom of this marketing by warm human contact. You've got to take the time to explain it, demonstrate it, and train people to do it. You may have to pop for a book or tape about memory improvement—to help your people memorize customer names.

Some may balk because it means a smidgeon of extra work. But it's still worth your time and effort to be sure the phone is answered with sincere friendliness, that each person who enters your store or office is made to feel like the most important customer ever, and that customers are nurtured, loved, treated with special handling.

The essence of guerrilla marketing is the expenditure of time, energy, and imagination rather than the investment of megabucks. How you say hello and good-bye takes little of any of those, yet it is a wonderful opportunity to practice the human kindness that is part of guerrilla marketing.

PUBLICITY CONTACTS

Why do you suppose it's so simple for some people to generate free publicity for their enterprises and so difficult for others?

The answer is in the name of this report. To attract publicity you must have news of interest to the readers or viewers of the media that will do the publicizing. But a fact of life is that you also should be personally acquainted with the media people in charge of selecting the stories to be covered. The more contacts, the more coverage.

Just who are the people you should know? Well, you can begin anywhere, but should end up knowing a full array of managing editors, feature editors, business editors, and any other editors who deal with your field—be it science, cars, computers, real estate, home services, or whatever.

It also helps if you know the owner of the newspaper, radio station, magazine. The closer the contact, the more coverage.

It's one thing to send a press release, fact sheet, and glossy black-and-white photo to someone by title, then sit back and pray. It's something else to send those same items to someone by name, then call the person and say, "Ellen, let's have lunch tomorrow. I want you to have the inside story on that PR stuff I sent earlier this week."

You can meet Ellens and their ilk by joining press clubs in your area and by joining other clubs to which they belong. Many successful guerrillas learn the restaurants and saloons frequented by these members of the fourth estate, then pop in, offering to buy a refreshment for their potential publicity contacts. Do you need several publicity contacts? Become a regular at the restaurant or saloon.

Urging you to do all in your power to meet the people who decide what gets covered and what doesn't is my main responsibility in this report. Your responsibility now is to meet them, get to know them on a first-name basis, feed them some good hard news to fascinate their readers. Make their jobs easier with your professionalism, then develop the news so you can take advantage of these contacts.

Unaggressive marketers do little or nothing to generate free publicity. Aggressive marketers regularly send out press releases. Guerrilla marketers regularly send out press releases to known publicity contacts, then call these contacts to be sure their story gets the proper attention.

Obtaining many publicity contacts is pure guerrilla marketing—because it involves an investment of time, energy, and imagination rather than the more costly investment of money. Do these contacts equate with profits? You bet they do! Are you willing to exert the time and energy to earn them?

BRAND-NAME AWARENESS

The *Harvard Business Review* warns the growing number of small business owners that there will be so many small businesses in the 1990s you'll have to develop your own brand name in order to succeed, then make people aware of that name.

If you're a true-blue guerrilla, you'd want that awareness regardless of what any publication says. Brand-name awareness equals credibility. Awareness of your brand usually means confidence in it, and confidence is the key to healthy sales.

Many people have purchased products or services simply because they were familiar with the name. They might have known zilch about the benefits or the price, but they bought anyhow. Being aware of the name was enough. Researchers asking "Why did you buy this product or service?" very frequently receive the answer "Because I heard of it." "Because I heard of it" is synonymous with brand-name awareness.

How does a company achieve brand-name awareness? By constant repetition of their name. This repetition can come via frequent advertising, constant exposure to a sign, consistent mailings, repeated stories in the newspaper or in other media, or a combination of all of these. This repetition not only results in brand-name awareness but also penetrates the unconscious minds of prospects. And that's where most purchase decisions are made. No wonder so many people buy things "because they heard of them."

People enjoy buying from friends. Frequent exposure to your name breeds a sense of familiarity that puts you almost into that lofty category of friend. It results in what is called "top-of-the-mind awareness." It creates the share of mind that must first precede a share of market.

Brand-name awareness of the highest quality is a lasting awareness. A person can read your ad, then be aware of your name for a week or two after reading it. After that, if they don't hear your name, chances are they'll forget it.

The key to lasting brand-name awareness comes with consistency. It's obvious that the more a person hears or reads your name, the more aware he or she will be of your name. Awareness does not automatically lead to sales. But if a person is going to buy something in your category of business, you've got a whopping advantage over any company of which they are not aware.

Guerrilla marketers aim to gain brand-name awareness as well as brand-benefit awareness. If customers know your name and the benefits of buying from you, you're in dandy shape. This awareness takes time, but is always worth the wait. So is anything else that ensures your very survival.

ENTHUSIASM

Enthusiasm is one of the most powerful of all 100 guerrilla marketing weapons. It proves beyond words that the product or service being marketed is worth getting excited about. It conveys an attitude that is highly contagious.

The contagion starts at top management. It then spreads to sales management. From here, this healthy contagion spreads throughout the sales department, then moves into the minds of prospects. If your offering lives up to your enthusiasm, the prospects become customers, catch it, and spread it to their friends. That enthusiasm is the energy that powers word-of-mouth advertising.

And the cost for all of this positivity about your product or service? Absolutely zero. Enthusiasm is an ultrapowerful motivator. And it's free. A very delightful and profitable combination.

It is simple for me to tell you about the power of honest enthusiasm. It is also simple for you to convey the attitude to your staff. It is similarly simple for everyone in your organization to be enthusiastic about a product, service, promotion, offer, price, new line, or virtually anything on a Monday morning—even a Monday afternoon.

But it is very difficult to maintain that enthusiasm all day every day. It is extremely difficult to maintain it throughout an entire sales force. Still, knowing how strongly it influences sales, efforts should be made to establish, then maintain, this enthusiasm.

How do you do it? You begin with high quality and real value—conditions that inspire sincere enthusiasm. Then you take that enthusiasm to new heights with a sales meeting. An enthusiastic person tells the staff why he or she is so darned enthusiastic. The person's natural enthusiasm is a plus. Background music certainly doesn't hurt. If ever there was a right time for a dog-and-pony show to inflame enthusiasm, this is it. Enthusiasm is maintained by regular brief meetings early each day, especially if you can report spectacular results from the day before.

The more your salespeople know about the benefits of your offering, the more enthusiastic they can be. So be sure that you communicate the benefits clearly and with flair.

Enthusiasm originates in the brain, but is conveyed by the heart. If you sense a lack of it, perhaps people didn't understand what all the fuss was about at the outset. Make sure everyone knows and that they are as excited as you are. You can succeed with the other 99 weapons, but if a prospect senses a lackluster attitude on the part of the salespeople, all that effort goes for naught. Enthusiasm is the weapon that adds firepower to all the others—and just when it counts.

COMPETITIVENESS

As you well know, there are 100 weapons in a guerrilla marketing arsenal. Your competitors are aware of perhaps 5 to 10 of these weapons. They are probably using between 3 to 5 of the weapons, possibly even fewer.

To a guerrilla, competitiveness means being aware of all 100 of the weapons and using 40 to 60 of them. You may not be able to fire up all 40 to 60 at once, but you can activate them on a regular basis until eventually you are using as much weaponry as possible—and using it properly.

Competitiveness means being aware of the brute force of marketing and the singular advantage that comes to those who are guerrillas. Constant improvement of marketing is another sign of competitiveness. Every direct mailing tests another idea. Every marketing effort is tracked. The annual guerrilla marketing calendar is followed and sharpened each year. Paying this close attention to marketing is a clear sign of competitiveness.

The best competitors do not react to their competition. They act in ways that force competitors to react to them. Competitiveness refers to an attitude rather than a personality. Many fierce competitors are soft-spoken, polite, quiet, self-effacing, courteous, and friendly. They prove their competitiveness in their work, not their words.

They love the competitive environment, and show it in their intense study of their product or service, their market, and their competition. Perhaps the single trait they share the most is their deep orientation to their customers.

Their commitment to customer service, customer follow-up, and customer benefits is what makes them competitive. They are patient, yet fierce in their ardor for the sale. They do not recognize the concept of failure. To them, people never fail; they only quit trying. So these people never quit trying. They are anxious to call up as many weapons as possible because they know this will benefit their prospects.

Is knocking the competition a sign of competitiveness? Of course not. In fact, the best competitors laud their competition, and in doing so rise above their competitors' level while gaining the respect of their prospects.

Being competitive is a nonstop job. Using all 100 weapons of guerrilla marketing, then allowing your energy to peter out, is not being competitive. True winners continue their attack, never letting up, always searching for new ways to market. Constant employment of a broad range of weaponry is the soul of competitiveness and of guerrilla marketing. If you're not sincerely excited at the prospect of being able to use a multitude of weapons, you're not really competitive enough to be a guerrilla.

5

WEAPONS OVERLOOKED BY NONGUERRILLAS

A slew of underestimated weapons can aid you in your quest for an honest buck. Most of these are so underestimated that they're not even considered by the people who run marketing programs for companies. Some may seem worthy expenditures of your time, but hardly part of marketing.

When evaluating these weapons for your own ends, keep in mind that there's a whale of a difference between simply doing the job and doing the job excellently. An article you write can be a onetime moment in the spotlight—or a twenty-year weapon, if it is liberally reprinted, included in all your print marketing, and used as a stepping-stone to gobs of free publicity. It's up to you whether the weapon fires a single bullet or salvo after salvo. It all comes down to the earnestness of your competitive spirit.

Mainstream companies generally employ traditional marketing methods. That's one reason they overlook the upcoming eighteen. Some marketing supervisors know some of these could be of immense help, but consider them nearly impossible to employ, such as a monthly column in a community or business publication (which is not all that difficult to arrange for your firm) or a testimonial letter from a key person or a big name company.

Like all guerrillas, you'll have to devote valuable time, energy, and imagination to these marketing efforts. Like all guerrillas, you'll barely be able to suppress a grin when you see the results you can achieve with them and the minuscule size of your financial investment.

More than half of the 18 weapons are free, or nearly free. The others are hardly budget-breakers. That's why entrepreneurs across the land are discovering, utilizing, and profiting from these overlooked marketing munitions.

The first, community involvement, is the most multifaceted, but can reap rich rewards beyond profits for your company.

Take-one boxes hold your brochure—one targeted at the people who frequent each placement site. Generally, the prospects identify themselves merely by taking a brochure in the first place.

Window displays are overlooked by most companies because few, except the retailers, have windows in which to display. But you'll find that many retailers will be more than happy to give you space in their windows in exchange for your helping them in some way.

Club and association memberships provide you with information, visibility, contacts, and an opportunity to prove what a conscientious person you are.

Team sponsorships increase a community's acceptance of you, even if your team has a losing record. Lots of teams are looking for sponsors like you. Lots of people will show up at games and read your name on a teamful of jerseys.

Advertisements and publicity stories pack a mean punch but are rarely, if ever, overlooked by a business owner. Reprints of those ads and publicity stories are overlooked. Reprints are almost as power-packed as the originals and come at a teensy-tiny fraction of the price—in money, time, energy, or imagination. If you haven't been availing yourself of these, but could, don't overlook them anymore.

If you have a sales force, sales training can work wonders for your sales and profits. But some kinds of sales training are a waste of time, while other kinds are marketing dynamite. I'm glad we'll have a chance to investigate why up ahead.

Circulars aren't free, but they cost only pennies apiece and they enable you to target your audience even better than the mass media. Can you imagine a Fortune 500 company including circulars in a marketing meeting?

How about refreshments? Although this is an effective guerrilla marketing weapon, I'd bet dollars (what you'll make) to doughnuts (what you'll serve) that you'll never read the word *refreshments* in a Fortune 500 firm's marketing plan.

If you can write a book or article on the topic of your business, you can turn either into a serious marketing thrust to gain credibility, confidence, and thereby, new profits. Just don't get carried away and write about your business. Stick to the big picture.

Perhaps you're not dazzled at the idea of writing something. That's OK. You can talk about it. A course or lecture on your topic will provide you with credibility and earn prospect confidence. Just think of the business you can generate if you can write *and* talk.

In my own life, which is divided into writing, speaking, and doing marketing, I find that the writing gets me speaking invitations and marketing assignments; the speaking gets me marketing assignments as well as aiding the sale of my books; the marketing gives me fodder for writing and talking.

I admit to offering no gift certificates, but I recommend that you give it some thought. Companies that didn't consider these weapons in the past are finding that they are a new and welcome source of sales. How can you lose?

Free and easy. That's what testimonials are. If someone compliments you on your products or services, ask if they'll put that into writing. Almost always, they will. Those testimonial letters can be merged with many of your other marketing weapons. Guerrillas never overlook so effective a weapon.

Tie-ins with others, also known as "fusion marketing," are a way of having your back scratched in return for scratching someone else's. It's just as simple to set up, and nearly as pleasurable. Read all about it, then do it, really go all out and do it.

You can pen a column for a publication and get regular exposure of your company name, and maybe even its phone and address. This is easier than you might think and well worth exploring. Ask any business owner who already has a column.

If you simply can't write a book, an article, or a column, certainly you can publish a newsletter. A zillion U.S. entrepreneurs have learned that the cost is lower than ever and the results are highly encouraging.

Classified ads are run in very well known marketing media, yet they are overlooked by the majority of business owners. These people think that classified sections are the same as they were twenty years ago. But these sections have changed. Their distribution has expanded. They deserve your attention. A faint smile comes to my face when I visualize the boardroom of a mega-conglomerate wherein classified ads are being discussed.

Posters are marketing weapons that are overlooked, often because of lack of imagination. But the visual impact of a poster and the low cost to create one from existing marketing materials should change the way you think about posters—what they show and where they are displayed.

Eighteen weapons are a lot to overlook. I'm glad you're taking the time to move these marketing opportunities from the fringes of your consciousness to the forefront—even if only for a few minutes. Already I imagine you can see how some of these should take on a more important role for your company.

I figure you're beginning to realize how low the cost

would be to add some of these to your permanent arsenal. Perhaps you won't use all of them, but even the addition of a few can make a big difference. And never are you asked to make a big investment. Rarely is the reward so happily out of proportion to the risk.

Call it guerrilla mathematics if you want.

COMMUNITY INVOLVEMENT

As I tend to remind you, people like to buy from friends. The more involved you are with the community, the more friends you will make. A deep and healthy relationship with the community is the key to many an entrepreneurial success.

Your involvement can take many forms. In each, you must be sincere, lest you be perceived as crass. For instance, it is good to join community organizations, but it is crass to join them solely to make contacts and not to work hard for them. It is good to sponsor a Little League or bowling team, but it is crass to attend no games.

Opportunities to market through the medium of the community are abundant. Here are ten that come to mind:

1. Develop a promotion involving a local school or college. Either demonstrate your product or service for a class or offer a discount to students through their newspaper.
2. Establish tie-ins with community stores. Offer to distribute their brochures if they'll distribute yours, to put up their sign if they'll put up yours, to include their circular in your next mailing if they'll include your circular in theirs.
3. If there are large businesses in your community, provide special discount cards for their employees.
4. Post your own sign or circular on local bulletin boards. Find them at supermarkets, general stores, churches, businesses, and clubs.
5. Offer your product or service to local charities as part of their fund-raising efforts. Ask nothing in return.
6. Donate your product or service to your community for use in a park or public place, where the community can benefit.

7. Support the local media—newspaper or radio—if feasible, and embed your name and benefits in the minds of the locals. Emphasize your localness in your marketing.
8. Make special offers, with mailings sent to clubs in your community: health, social, service, recreational.
9. Organize community events such as 10K races, essay contests, or painting contests. Give T-shirts to participants.
10. Drive through your community spotting other ways you can serve it, other entities with whom you can tie in.

Your community needs any support you can give it. While you're working at it, you'll find loads of chances to make friends and profits.

Take-One Boxes

For decades, guerrilla marketers have distributed their sales literature, usually in the form of a brochure or coupon, through individual retailers and on public transit systems.

They realized excellent returns for their efforts, as you can, too. Take-one boxes are placed at strategic locations where your prospects are likely to be found. Here are five reasons to employ this guerrilla marketing weapon, if it is feasible for your operation:

1. The cost is very low. Take-one boxes deliver your message for just pennies per exposure, based upon participating retailers' average customer count of 3,650 people per month per store. Compare this with direct mail, which costs at least 90 percent more than take-one boxes.

2. They reach people in a buying mood. Direct mail often is considered junky or time-consuming or intrusive, putting people in a resistant mental state. Take-one boxes, because they offer data on a voluntary basis, do not alienate people and are seen by folks in a receptive frame of mind. These people actually want to read what you have to say.

3. Take-one boxes are scientifically accountable. You learn how they're working and where they're working. By careful tracking, you can get a complete report on how much of your literature was taken from each store. You'll learn where your prospects live and shop. You'll know if your coupon offers or brochures are up to snuff.

4. You'll benefit from the billboard effect of take-one boxes. Even those people who do not take one of what you are offering for free will see your name again and again. Trying to get that exposure with advertising or direct mail costs two arms and six legs.

5. You'll be utilizing a marketing weapon that is probably overlooked by your competitors. After all, they are not as aware of the 100 guerrilla marketing weapons as you are, and they're probably using just a handful. By using take-one boxes, you are operating with a more complete arsenal.

The keys to succeeding with this weapon are selecting locations that seem appropriate for box placement, using their ability to reach serious prospects as your criteria, figuring how to distribute brochures to the empty boxes in an economical and efficient manner, fabricating the boxes themselves, creating the right brochures, and deciding how to monitor your efforts.

You'll find that as you experiment with this weapon, you'll get better and better at all the keys to success. And, like most guerrilla marketing, the task will get easier and easier.

WINDOW DISPLAYS

Window displays offer a marketing strength possessed by few other weapons: They generate impulse purchases. Keep this in mind when planning your offerings, your design, your copy, and your overall themes.

Also keep in mind the direction from which your main traffic is coming, and aim your marketing right between their eyes. Say something of interest to them. Intrigue them. Make them a tempting offer. Don't just use your windows as a general display. Bring them to life.

Can you use your windows to put on a live demonstration? Can you bolster their effectiveness by introducing a unique feature such as two pussycats? A video of your benefits? Five simultaneous videos of your benefits? A framed testimonial letter? A reprint of a full-page ad run in *Time* magazine? (In a local edition, the price is much lower than you'd guess.) A person working hard while using what you sell? There's no rule that says windows must be static.

Window displays don't have to be limited to your windows only. You can arrange cooperative ventures with nearby—or even distant—business owners who have windows with display opportunities.

For example, arrange for them to display your wares or even your sign in exchange for your including their brochure in your next mailing. In this way, it is possible to have many local window displays. As in all guerrilla marketing, it takes merely time, energy, and imagination. Such marketing does not call for big budgets.

Change your basic window display on a regular basis to keep your whole operation feeling and looking fresh. True guerrillas change at least one element every day to offer new items to regular passersby. Unlike mass-media marketing, where repetition is your ally, in window displays repetition forces lost interest.

Window displays work best when combined with TV, radio, and/or newspaper advertising to communicate your theme. Your windows should capitalize on the momentum these media generate with enticing offers to come on in *now*.

Depending on the size of your window, always remember to brightly illuminate your display, clearly (referring to size of type and typography selected) state your message, and most important, center your display or displays on core ideas. These ideas should offer benefits at a value.

If you have a small window, you'll probably display one theme idea. If you have a huge window, five displays might beckon to those who pass. Always use the theme as a bridge to your entire selection. Avoid appearing limited.

CLUB AND ASSOCIATION MEMBERSHIPS

Many guerrillas secure all the business they need simply by joining social clubs, country clubs, service clubs, professional clubs, health clubs, trade associations, and the many other organizations that exist to serve our herd instinct.

A few of the joiners belong to a plethora of clubs. Some join but one. A few of the joiners do little more than add their names to the club roster. Some of the joiners knock themselves out with work in an effort to improve their club and its value to members.

A clear fact of life in business is that people like to buy from people with whom they are familiar. Another clear fact is that you can make a whole lot of friends when you join clubs and associations.

If you join with solely that mind-set, many club members will see through your motives and become anything but your friends. But if you join with the idea of working hard for the club, the members will appreciate your devotion and conscientiousness. You can't blame them for assuming you exert those same attributes in business. You can't blame them for wanting to become your customers.

The joining of clubs and associations provides many benefits to the success-oriented guerrilla:

1. You meet a lot of prospects.
2. You meet a lot of referrers.
3. You meet a lot of suppliers.
4. You meet a lot of fellow guerrillas with whom you can network or form a loose alliance.
5. You learn which customers are unhappy.
6. You learn of coming industry advancements.
7. You have access to other companies' grapevines.
8. You can become close friends with honest prospects.
9. You can intensify relationships with customers.

10. You can make a contribution to your industry or to your community.

That's a lot of good things, especially considering their cost.

Joining clubs and associations is rarely considered marketing, in the way newspaper ads and signs are considered marketing. But more deals are closed on golf courses, in card rooms, and in club rooms than you might imagine.

A final note: If you work hard to deserve to be elected to a high post, especially president, of your club or organization, it will increase your identity of expertise, authority, efficiency, and visibility to make a dramatic impact upon your business, possibly even your career.

Team Sponsorships

Whether your company is one of the proud sponsors of the United States Olympic Team or an equally proud sponsor of a local Little League team, the benefit to you is the same: involvement with your target audience.

In many communities, sponsorship of a baseball team; bowling team; basketball, football, soccer, or drum-and-bugle team is the key to a closer relationship with the community as a whole—and with the movers and shakers within it.

Certainly, the presence of your name on the jerseys of a team won't win new customers all by itself. But it will help create the marketing momentum that leads to the eventual sale—if it is part of a well-stocked and actively utilized guerrilla marketing arsenal.

When you sponsor a team, you get to meet customers and prospects in a business-free environment. You can become friends with them—if you want. You can demonstrate your conscientiousness in the way you support your team.

People will assume you apply this same conscientiousness to your business. They will gain confidence in you.

Word of warning: Whatever you do, do not sponsor a team if you will not actively support it. That means showing up for games, cheering at appropriate moments, and doing what you can to help the team become champions. If you sponsor a team and do not do these things, the community will probably recognize it as the shallow act it is, and your attempt at marketing through community involvement will backfire.

Sponsoring a team is a way to meet prospects, intensify relationships with customers, get your company's name in the local newspaper (hopefully as the sponsor of winners), and become known as part of the community. It is a way to make friends.

All along your company will be gaining crucial ground in the minds of your prospects. It is a marketing truism that people tend to patronize businesses with which they are familiar. Your sponsoring of a team or two—and rooting for your players—will automatically make your prospects more familiar with your company. Or will it? Sponsoring a team doesn't always make sense.

Sponsoring a team makes a lot of sense if your prospects share your interest in the league. If they don't, your sponsorship will be more for personal joy than for marketing success.

But if key prospects will be out there rooting with—or against—your team, you might find that sponsoring a team is every bit as effective as running a national TV commercial.

Reprints of Ads and Publicity

Guerrillas see to it that many of their advertisements and publicity stories do double, even triple duty.

Here's what they do: They have reprints made, by the publication or by a copy shop, of their ads and PR stories. Some of the reprints are printed on standard 8½-by-11-inch paper. Some are printed on cardboard stock with a border and are destined for display on an easel or in a window.

Some guerrillas reprint their ads—or stories—all the way up to the size of a five-foot sign. Shops specializing in photo blowups can handle that job with aplomb. And they can do it economically.

One of the drawbacks to a PR story is that it appears but once. This is not true if guerrillas mail reprints of the story, give reprints away in their store or place of business, put reprints up in prominent places where the right people, their target audience, can read them.

One of the drawbacks to an ad is the cost. This doesn't stop guerrillas who post large reprints of their ads on their front door, within their store, or anyplace else that makes sense. They give reprints to customers. They know that ad reprints are a boon for word-of-mouth marketing.

Some, with good-looking or highly informative reprints, frame them and hang them proudly on the premises. Some use their ad reprints as sales tools so that salespeople can put them to work as sales aids. They know that points made to the eye are 68 percent more effective than points made to the ear.

Being true guerrillas, they make their points to both. And reprints are part of their arsenal.

When you have enough ad and publicity reprints, you can put them together into a press kit or sales kit. Unlike many types of marketing, which lose their zip after time, gobs of reprints gain zip because they add up to credibility.

It doesn't matter that the story was published in 1965 or that the ad ran in 1966.

What does matter is the cumulative effect of seeing all those reprints at one time. It makes your business appear as part of the local—or national—scene. This builds consumer confidence. And confidence breeds sales, as if you didn't know.

Do you reprint everything? No. But you should reprint a lot of things. The cost is amazingly low and the effectiveness is high. As marketing weapons, reprints rank exceptionally high as a downright value. And guerrillas, like other human beings, are always grateful for a value.

SALES TRAINING

In my own experience, I've always seen a clear cause and effect between sales training and sales. The more sales training, the higher the sales. It's that simple.

Sales training should be repeated regularly. Sales reps should receive it by audiotape, videotape, in person, by role-playing, and in seminars. Because the very top sales-people in the country use special words and phrases, the best sales training is a memorized sales pitch. And my personal favorite among sales training aids is an audiotape of a company salesperson making a successful sale using the right words, phrases, and voice inflections. The 80 percent of a sales force that produces only 20 percent of the sales can learn a heck of lot from this tape.

The sales pitch should be so well memorized that it does not seem memorized. But only through memorization will the key words and phrases be used every time—and every time is probably when they should be used.

Along with words and phrases, sales training should attempt to convey a sense of enthusiasm. This generally occurs when the sales staff learns the maximum about their product or service, when they compare their offering with others, and when they have an in-depth understanding of the marketplace, the competition, and their target audience. Sales training should never fail to discuss these items in detail. The more a salesperson knows, the better he or she can sell.

Sales training can come from a sales manager, a president, a top salesperson, or a professional sales trainer. My recommendation is to try all of those entities so that you can learn which motivates your sales force the best.

You might consider buying proven audiotapes or videotapes to improve your sales training. The person who conducts the sessions should be not only a great salesperson, but a topflight trainer as well. The trainer must have the gift of being able to repeat topics week in and week out without losing the audience, dampening enthusiasm, or creating disharmony.

One of the most endearing qualities of sales training is how easily measurable it is. Conduct it, then see if sales are up. If not, they should be. Perhaps salespeople should be supplied audiotapes to hear while driving. Perhaps some of them need special tutoring. Whatever they need, give it to them, because sales training will serve as the life force of your business.

Summarizing points about sales training:

1. Keep it clear.
2. Keep it interesting.
3. Relate it to each salesperson's income.
4. Keep it up.

Circulars

Circulars are far less expensive to produce than brochures. They contain a lot less information and give you a great deal of flexibility. Besides being distributable at your own place of business, they can be handed out on street corners, placed under windshield wipers, distributed at other business owners' places of business, and posted as signs.

A quick printer ought to be able to produce circulars for you at a cost of only a few cents each. The prime idea of a circular is to make an offer and give the highlights of doing business with you. Of course, it should also have your address, phone number, credit cards accepted (if any), hours, and theme line.

Although no rule says printing on colored paper is better than printing on white paper, you do have the flexibility of using colored paper at no additional cost. Just be sure you use an ink color that is easily readable on the color you choose.

The main thrust of a circular should be a clear and simple offer—using a headline. Although visual support always helps, many successful circulars use no artwork or photos at all. If you are considering circulars, consider all the places at which they may be circulated: on bulletin boards throughout your community, as part of one of your mailings, as part of someone else's mailing, as a self-mailer, as a bag stuffer, as an insert in a newspaper, in shopping centers and sporting events, at trade shows (directing people to your booth or promoting a specific offering)—the list is limited only by your imagination.

Often, the design for a circular is provided for free by the printer. That helps keep costs even lower. The printer may have several good ideas based on successful circulars he or she has printed for others. Tap into that experience if you can. Don't forget, you don't have to flag attention with a circular; you already have it. You can get right down to the business of selling.

Tell cooperating businesses in your locality that you'll distribute their circulars if they'll distribute yours. Insert a circular along with all items that you sell—offering something else for sale. Post your circular in your window if it does not interfere with your window display. And have a generous supply of extra circulars on hand for customers who do not yet know of your special offer. Keep them by the cash register.

The keys to successful circulars are:

1. Simplicity of offer
2. Timeliness of offer
3. Economy of production
4. Flexibility of use
5. Clarity of information
6. Tie-in with your current identity

No wonder many small business owners consider circulars to be one of the most guerrillalike of all the media.

Refreshments

I once addressed the national convention of a large cooperative, attended by about 300 members. The cooperative was in the business of supplying parts and equipment to people in the maintenance trades: builders, plumbers, electricians, repair people of all types.

During my presentation, I told the group that there are 100 guerrilla marketing weapons. Then I listed all 100 weapons. When I completed my talk, I asked if anyone in the audience utilized an effective guerrilla marketing weapon that I had not mentioned.

A hand went up in the rear of the auditorium. When I asked the person holding up his hand what weapon he successfully employed, he said, "Coffee and fresh doughnuts." He went on to explain that his customers come to him very early in the morning to stock up on the parts they'll be needing. He told the audience and the newly enlightened speaker that since word of his coffee and doughnuts spread through town, his business was the best it had ever been. He then asked if that was a genuine marketing weapon.

I'll say it is! If it attracts new prospects, satisfies old customers, and generates more business, it is a dandy marketing weapon. Just because it is overlooked by most authorities (including me) doesn't mean it is not part of the marketing process. To him, it was a crucial part. "Pulls in more customers than my advertising," he added.

If you can attract new (and qualified) prospects, satisfy old customers, and generate more business by serving coffee, tea, soft drinks, cheese, cookies, doughnuts, candy, apples, or any type of refreshment—give it careful thought. The cost will be very low; the payoff can be high. Wine might also be a proper refreshment, but it crosses over into a new and ticklish territory, so I'd treat the serving of any alcoholic beverage with extreme care.

The whole concept is to make yours a pleasant place to be, to provide the best possible service to prospects and customers, to treat them as humans and not just sources of revenue, and to utilize nontraditional methods of marketing if they seem appropriate to you and appealing to your target market.

Many a bookstore has a coffee nook. Many a styling salon serves fruit juices and soft drinks. Auto service facilities are learning of the goodwill they gain by giving away coffee and pastries. The whole idea of sharing or providing food and drink is an idea about intensifying the human bond—and that's always smart.

Give thought to what types of refreshments your prospects and customers might enjoy, whether the refreshments are appropriate, and how soon you can serve them, and see for yourself the marketing benefits they can bring to you.

BOOKS AND ARTICLES

As all guerrillas well know, the more credibility you have, the more confidence your prospects will have in your business—magically transforming them into customers.

Of the many ways to gain this confidence, one of the least costly and most enjoyable is writing books on your topic of expertise, or if you wish to take a shortcut to credibility, writing articles for magazines and newspapers.

To do either a book or an article requires three things from you—or a willing ghostwriter:

1. Researching the material to be covered
2. Organizing the material to be written
3. Writing the book or article

A fourth effort is usually required, but can be surmounted: publishing your book or article. Prospects aren't as impressed at manuscripts as they are at printed words.

If you can't find a publisher to put out your book or a publication to publish your article, do it yourself.

Self-publish your book. It can cost you anywhere from a few hundred to a few thousand dollars, but it can generate credibility worth far in excess of that.

The completed book can still be sold in stores, still reviewed by the newspapers (good luck), and still bestow upon you the trappings of a proven authority.

Desktop-publish your article. Or ask a local computer whiz to create a newsletter for you. You can write all the articles or you can write only one of them, using material from others to complete the newsletter, which can be as brief as two pages. There will be more about newsletters in a few pages. Still, I want to make the point that when printed words, many of them in fact, appear beneath your name, you become an instant and an automatic authority in your field.

I've had the good fortune of gaining not only the credibility of books and articles but also the income that is often, but not always, a concomitant of such efforts. Perhaps it will work out the same way for you. But that should not be your prime purpose. Your prime goal is to prove your expertise by penning a published work.

Gold-medal guerrillas use their published works as lethal weapons in their marketing arsenals, including reprints of their articles and offers of their free books in direct mailings. The lives of these weapons are long and productive.

And the rewards often far transcend mere financial gain.

COURSES AND LECTURES

To establish yourself as an authority in your field, consider giving courses or delivering lectures on your topic of expertise.

Many community colleges and university extension centers would love to have someone teach a course the school does not yet offer but that would be of interest to the community in general. They also would like it if the teacher were a person from the real world rather than the academic world. Consider doing this. It proves that you're an expert and it puts a few extra bucks in your pocket.

Forget those extra bucks and offer your services as a speaker for one of the many clubs in your area. These clubs meet regularly and often engage the services of a speaker. If you offer your services free—and your topic is of interest to the audience—you can engage in pure guerrilla marketing. Spend zero while wooing many.

There are five important points to remember if you're to offer courses and lectures on your topic. All five are tied for first place in importance. Let's examine them:

1. Don't use your teaching forum as a place from which you may hawk your products or services. People are there to be told, not sold. So—sell nothing; simply give great and valuable information away for free.
2. Don't attempt to lecture or give a course unless you are a clear and dynamic speaker. A boring speaker can turn off as many people as he or she can turn on. As always, quality counts; if you offer it, your audience will assume your company offers it.
3. Use visual aids whenever possible. It is not in bad taste to use aids that promote your own product or service— just as long as they are there to explain, not coerce.
4. Give your company phone number, verbally and visually, so that people can contact you for further information. If you're good while you speak, they will.

5. Always think in terms of your audience—not your company or yourself. Knock yourself out giving that audience important and esoteric data so as to underscore your expertise and to please the audience.

It is possible to market to thousands of people through courses and lectures without spending one cent. I've been doing it for about a decade and I recommend it highly as a pure and amazingly cost-effective method of guerrilla marketing.

If you teach courses and give lectures on your field of expertise, use audiotapes of your presentations as a marketing device. And milk your expertise for all the PR you can.

GIFT CERTIFICATES

If you think that gift certificates are the domain of department stores and no one else, you are not a true-blue guerrilla. More and more marketing guerrillas are learning that gift certificates work in virtually any business. And they work especially well in businesses where gift certificates have not ever been offered.

The reason for this is that offering gift certificates plants ideas in the minds of your prospects and in the minds of their friends.

It is difficult to select a gift for many people, especially if you purchase a gift or two for them each year. By giving them a gift certificate for something you know they will value, you'll be providing them with something that is both unique and desirable—a lovely combination.

To offer gift certificates, first prepare a series of small signs that say "Ask about our gift certificates." Then print up a quantity of actual gift certificates. It's nice if they are printed on parchment-type paper, but any fine paper stock will do.

Put the name of your company at the top of the certificate, leave room for the dollar amount, and leave room for the name of the recipient and the person authorized to sign the certificate. That person is probably you.

In your advertising, brochures, and in all marketing in which it is feasible, say these words: "Ask about our gift certificates." When people actually do ask, and they will, tell them the certificates are available in any amount (though $10 is a standard minimum amount) and that they are good for anything you sell. They should not have a cutoff date. After all, they are gifts.

You'll be amazed at the amount of people who actually do ask about your gift certificates, and you'll be delighted at the number of people who purchase them. They make perfect gifts, are always affordable, and are almost always appreciated. I can't think of when they wouldn't be.

Gift certificates do not work a whit unless you announce their availability—especially at gift-giving times such as Christmas, Mother's Day, and Valentine's Day. Still, they work all year long—if you let your public know that you offer them.

Hint: Add a few testimonials about your gift certificates to your brochures or your next direct mailing. That will make the gift certificates work even harder, and more people than usual will purchase them.

People are often looking for unusual gift ideas. A gift certificate for what you sell may be just the ticket for them.

TESTIMONIALS

Testimonials are used less than they ought to be, yet they're far more effective than many people think they are. I'm not talking about celebrity testimonials. Anyone can buy one of those. This is a report for guerrillas.

So this report is about the kind of testimonials that don't cost one penny—yet are incredibly effective anyhow. This kind of testimonial comes from your customers. The best kinds come from people like:

George C. Anderson, CPA
Columbia, South Carolina

The worst kind come from people like:

C.W.S.
Texas

You can use testimonials in a variety of wonderful ways. All are effective. All are inexpensive. One way is to make copies of the testimonials and make them part of a mailing package. Another way is to use the testimonial, or part of it, in an ad. A third way is to post the actual testimonial letters within your place of business. A fourth, and quite common, way is to publish several of the testimonials as part of a customer brochure.

Some guerrillas paper a wall of their reception area with testimonial letters. Others frame a few and proudly display them. The idea is to show them to as many people as possible. Naturally, they make ultrapowerful tools for your salespeople.

When prospects see all those testimonials, especially those from people to whom they can relate, they gain confidence in you. They're less worried about making an error by buying what you sell.

There are three basic ways to obtain testimonials:

1. Pray that you get some.
2. Ask satisfied customers for some.
3. Be prepared for the satisfied customer who will ask you to write it, then he or she will sign it.

All three are perfectly valid yet frequently overlooked ways of proving that others have loved what you sell.

If you can get a testimonial on a fancy letterhead—the White House comes to mind, but IBM would do nicely—it will carry even more weight in influencing your prospects.

And of course you know that the more testimonials you have, the better. Doesn't even matter how old the testimonials are. Simply realize that they are more believable than ads, yet far more inexpensive. Just a guerrilla's cup of tea.

TIE-INS WITH OTHERS

One of the most rewarding, inexpensive, underused, and effective methods of marketing is to tie in your marketing efforts with the efforts of others.

An example of this might be to visit stores in a shopping mall and offer to distribute their brochures in your place of business or in your mailings. In return, all they've got to do is make your brochures available in their place of business, to put up signs for your business in theirs, and/or to include brochures for your business in their mailings.

Naturally, this works best if your two businesses are in some way complementary. But that is not even necessary. The idea is for each of you to help in cutting marketing costs for the other while helping to do more marketing.

You can discover a whole world of tie-in possibilities if you walk the commercial streets in your community, drive through the neighborhoods, study the local newspapers, peruse the yellow pages, or simply watch the local media. If tie-ins are on your mind, tie-in possibilities will appear all over the place.

I have a client who took in more than six figures in profits simply by offering to include another company's brochures with each order he filled. Because the brochures were coded, it was easy to trace sales to my client, who received a 15 percent cut of each sale. That 15 percent, over the course of a year, translated to over $100,000. The company with which he tied in was delighted to pay the $100,000 because the tie-in enabled them to cut marketing costs.

Cooperative marketing tie-ins can be accomplished with shared advertising costs, group promotions, or "I'll scratch your back [put up your sign in my window] if you'll scratch mine [put up my sign in your window]."

As you might expect, the deeper the tie-in, the greater

the payoff. Having someone put a pile of your brochures on their counter is one thing. Having their people recommend your place of business is considerably better. You can get that job done simply by handing cards to the referrers. Ask them to have their customer hand a card to you. You pay them a small fee for each card handed to you. Everyone ends up gaining: The customer learns of a new place to buy whatever it is you sell, you gain, the tie-in business gains, and the referrer gains. Most amazing, all this gain took place at a barely noticeable cost.

In Japan, all this is known as "fusion marketing." Incredibly diverse companies cooperate in ambitious and successful promotions at a fraction of what it would cost to do alone.

That's why tie-ins with others are one of the most guerrillalike of all marketing tactics. That's why I recommend it so highly. And so do many of my clients.

COLUMN IN A PUBLICATION

There are many newspapers in your locality—from metropolitan region to neighborhood. There are many magazines in your industry—from old and established to new and pioneering. And of course, there are newsletters.

Offer to write a regular column for one of the newspapers, if that's what your prospects read, or one of the magazines, if that's the best place to talk to your prospects. The best publication in which to advertise is generally the best for which to pen a column. And don't forget the newsletters.

Don't ask for money for your column—which should be weekly or monthly. Instead, ask to be given a byline at the top of the column, plus a sentence at the bottom that identifies your company and gives its address and phone number. Even getting one or two out of those three isn't bad.

You'll be happily surprised at the willingness of the publications to publish your column regularly—as long as it is interesting for the readers of the paper, as well as informative and well written. If it's good enough, it could be published in more than one publication.

If you're not a good enough writer, but you have the right information, consider working with a ghostwriter. Find one in the magazine *Writer's Digest*. Want to do it yourself? Write a one-page overview of a column, a one-page description of why you should be the columnist, and enclose four sample columns. If the columns deserve to be printed, this will prove it.

A column will establish you to your prospects as an expert, an authority, a source of news, a person in whom they can be confident. And a column can do this without costing you one red cent.

Better still, a column can give you your writing jollies and provide that deep inner satisfaction of being published.

While you're feeling warm inside, your prospects are feeling impressed. So they'll be more likely to feel positively inclined about your offers. Make those offers on all battle-fronts.

Just in case prospects missed your columns, there's no law against enclosing reprints of them in your mailings.

The columns must do absolutely no touting of your skills. Be sure not to look on them as advertisements. Don't sell a thing. Instead, give solid, substantial data that is clear and proves beyond words that you're the company with which to do business. Let your abilities tout themselves.

A client of mine received so much business from his column in a small newspaper that he cancelled his advertising there. This did not make the newspaper publisher happy, but it did wonders for my client's favorite line—the bottom line.

Newsletters

I've got to flat out recommend this guerrilla marketing weapon to you because newsletters have five spectacular advantages over most of the other marketing media:

1. They are amazingly flexible.
2. They are inexpensive to produce but effective to use.
3. They establish you as an authority.
4. They can be desktop-published.
5. They can become a profit center of their very own.

Right now, let's talk about newsletters as guerrilla marketing weapons rather than capitalist profit centers; though they do a sterling job as both, and one fine day you may decide to convert your marketing newsletter to an information-for-sale newsletter.

As a marketing tool, a newsletter proves your expertise. Everyone knows that words that appear in print are the truth, and that people who write them know the truth. You and I really know the truth, but let's not spoil the illusion.

A newsletter also makes a dandy direct-mail piece, a perfect medium for keeping in constant contact with your customers and your prospects, a dynamic tool for attracting new business, a stepping-stone to speaking invitations at events that can result in new business, and an impetus to write a book that would further underscore your genius while contributing to your cash flow.

Newsletters allow you to hear from and answer your customers. They allow you to strengthen the bond between you and the people even vaguely interested in you. And they increase the confidence level in you—an omnipotent benefit.

The best newsletters are short—the prime reason newsletters were invented in the first place. Make yours four or eight pages. Give a lot of information. But give it in short paragraphs. Use short sentences. Use short words. Tell people news, things they want to know but don't.

Have several people write the newsletter so that a selection of styles keeps it readable. Mail it monthly if you can, six times yearly if you can't, not fewer than four times yearly if you don't want to kid yourself that you've got a newsletter.

Make liberal use of the graphic capabilities of computers when publishing your newsletter. You can show items of interest to your readers plus items of sales persuasion for your company. You can demonstrate with photos, graphs, diagrams, and drawings. Do what you can to get readers to look forward to receiving your newsletter. Accomplish that and you're a guerrilla hero. Although newsletters should primarily give information, do not feel guilty for trying to make sales, win new customers, and gain referrals. There are four key words in publishing a newsletter: *news, deadline, reliable*, and *readable*. Hope your fifth word is *fun*.

Classified Ads

Classified ads are used by more guerrillas than any other marketing media. They are relatively inexpensive, amazingly flexible, available in media ranging from local newspapers to national magazines, free to produce, easy to change, and remarkably productive.

Because they reach serious prospects, since browsers rarely browse through the classified section, classified ads are often the ticket to a sale. To use them properly, first see where your competition uses them. That's often a good place to start because your prospects already know that's the right place to look for offerings such as yours.

I advise you to check the local newspapers to see the new classified sections that continously pop up. I know of antique dealers who get better results from inexpensive classified ads under "Antiques" than from expensive display ads in the same newspaper. I know a book publisher who enjoyed a higher response from his classified ad in *Psychology Today* than from his far more expensive display ad in the same publication. Booksellers advertise selected computer books in the "Computers" classified section. A serious reading of the classifieds is a good education in the media.

Your ad can stand out if it is worded in human being terms rather than in classified ad terms. You may end up paying for one extra line of space, but your sales can easily cover that cost.

Avoid being clever, cute, or fancy. Give the facts and be sure you are giving them ultraclearly. Even though many people will read your ad, act as though only one person will read it. The more one-on-one your ad sounds, the more sales it will attract. Put your headline into all capital letters or boldface type or both—to catch your prospects' attention. But don't put your entire ad into capital letters or you'll lose readership. Use a minimum amount of punctuation, especially exclamation marks.

To learn the most about classified ads, write for a free subscription to *Classified Communications*, 33 East Minor Street, Emmaus, PA 18049. This newsletter is published by magazine publishers who want you to enjoy the maximum number of sales from classified ads, so they give sage advice. And they counsel you to run your classified ad on a consistent basis rather than on an infrequent or hit-and-miss basis. They also advise you to let people order by phone, even to acquire a toll-free number if it's economically feasible. They also strongly advise you to accept credit cards.

Be sure you communicate price, benefits, and whether you offer a guarantee. Key words to use are: *you, free, new, right, fun, value, right, reliable, proven,* and *benefits*. And whatever you do, knock yourself out to be believable. It's always worth the effort. Check out the classified sections of magazines as well as newspapers. More and more magazines now have them. To a guerrilla, classified ads are always worth testing.

Posters

Posters have high impact because of their sheer size. If you have the ability to create or direct the creation of a handsome enough poster, you can mail it to people who will hang and even frame it because of its artistic merit.

Although full-color posters have a great deal of visual kick, you can get the same benefits from black and white or black and white plus one or two colors.

Guerrillas find the fodder for their posters in a wide variety of places. Some commission an artist or photographer to do an original poster. Others use a panel from their brochures. Still others use a photo or illustration from their ads. Some use materials supplied by their suppliers. And others purchase the rights to existing photos or art.

Posters can be displayed in a variety of venues: your store, your office, the stores or offices of your customers or prospects, in stores of merchants with whom you have a tie-in, in windows, on buildings, on posterboards, in airports, in schools, at clubs, in employee cafeterias, in rest rooms, in wind shelters, in bus stations, in subways, and any other place you can dream up. Many possibilities exist.

Just what should you say and show on a poster? You should *say* little and *show* as much as possible.

The impact for which you must aim is visual impact, not verbal impact. If you can add one or two words to enhance your visual message, by all means do so. But realize that posters are far more of a visual than a verbal marketing medium.

The placement of your poster within your store, if you have one, is critical. It will be competing for customer attention with your merchandise and store decor. Remember that when you put it in a high-visibility or low-visibility area. A changing room would be ideal for a clothing store, because posters can merchandise the things that people came in to buy as well as the things people did not come in to buy. Behind the cash register does both jobs very well.

Some space designers believe that posters should be put up at a slight slant to gain more impact. Some space owners invest in good frames for their posters. Still others put them on freestanding easels for maximum flexibility.

If you have a physical presence for your business, a place visited by customers and likely customers, or if these people congregate in a place that has space for a poster, give serious consideration to using this powerful visual method of marketing through the eyes rather than the ears.

It's possible to create a poster attractive enough to offer as a free gift in your advertising. Make that your guerrilla goal.

6
WEAPONS THAT MAKE YOU EASY TO BUY FROM

The information in this chapter is so important to both of us that I have added to my original seven-word guerrilla marketing credo an eighth word, also ending in *ent*, as do the other words.

The credo is now: commitment, investment, consistent, confident, patient, assortment, subsequent, and *convenient*. See to it that you comprehend the significance of these words, and that your company practices their principles, as described in *Guerrilla Marketing Attack*, to reap the profits of state-of-the-moment marketing.

Who would think that being convenient would entail using weapons? You probably associate the whole idea of using weapons with the idea of fighting. Keep thinking that way; you're fighting for new and long-term customers. Your competitors are fighting to take them away from you.

As a guerrilla, using the process of marketing with unconventional means, you should also associate the idea of weapons with caring.

Care about what customers have to go through in order

to buy what you're selling. Care about how easy it is for them to hear about you, to know what you have for sale, to phone you, to write to you, to find you, to make an intelligent purchase decision about what you offer, to try your offering, to trust you enough to risk making a mistake by purchasing, to buy your offering, to pay for it, to take delivery of it, then to explain their purchase to others.

People are more aware of their time right now than at any time in history. This survey result was reported in cover articles in major newspapers throughout the nation. The lack of time was reported by market researchers and poll takers from the University of Pennsylvania to the University of Maryland, from pollster Lou Harris to the Gallup Poll.

To a guerrilla marketer, that's a clear signal that people do not like waiting around, do not like difficulty in making a purchase, do not like doing business with companies that waste their time. Instead, people want to lead a more streamlined life. And you've got to cater to that goal.

Twist yourself into a pretzel making your company easy to do business with. Easy for customers, suppliers, service providers—heck, even for the IRS.

For starters, consider how you might say yes to every question posed by every prospect or customer. That's going to be impossible, but you'll be able to say the happy word in 75 percent of the cases. The more you say yes, the easier you are to buy from.

There are at least 9 weapons available to guerrillas in the quest for many and delighted customers. If you try all 9, I won't be surprised if you invent another 9—just because you see the positive effect of this type of weaponry. Tap your own buying experiences: Haven't some been more pleasant than others? Haven't some been actually dismal? What made them that way? What can you do to increase the joy for your customers as they contribute to your coffers?

You can stay open longer. That's one way of making you easier to buy from. It doesn't have to be you at the helm, but someone should be there to make it easier to buy.

You can be open more days. This will eventually make you a favorite of many customers, simply because up until you extended your days, buying what you sell was a hassle.

You can accept credit cards. Sure, most people have the two major credit cards, but many people are dangerously close to their credit limits. That's why increasing numbers of businesses accept at least five major credit cards.

You can make financing terms available. Even if this is rare in your business, do it. If it is common, stress it. Tell people how very easy it is to pay you.

You can put all of your offerings into a catalog. This gives prospects a better idea of your selection and offers more convenience. Catalogs don't have to be colorful, fancy, or expensive—as you'll see later in the chapter. By the way, people love to buy from catalogs.

You can give away free samples of your product or service. There's not much that can convince people of your quality more than the real goods. So if you can give them away—even teensy bits of them—know that this guerrilla marketing weapon is packed with dynamite.

You can offer people the convenience of a toll-free phone number. This makes it fast, easy, and inexpensive to contact you. It won't be all that inexpensive for you, but you won't mind the cost in the light of the results.

You can do what is necessary and advisable to muster up the maximum credibility. The more you have, the easier it will be to make the decision to buy from you. You'll appreciate some of the upcoming shortcuts to credibility.

You can populate the planet with satisfied customers. These are the living, breathing weapons who can take you up to guerrilla Nirvana. By being an easy company to buy from, you attract and keep these beloved creatures.

Because business owners who employ these weapons report glowing results in the form of increased profits, I heartily recommend learning all you can about all 9 weapons, then going all out to employ them.

Along with these major weapons of convenience come a host of smaller, but no less important ones:

- Be sure your business forms are written clearly.
- Do what you can to have bright lighting.
- Let signs enlighten people who visit you.
- Try to arrange ample parking for customers.
- Set yourself up to fax data to prospects.
- Communicate with customers by fax or computer modem.
- List your business where your prospects can find it.
- Impart information to callers on telephone hold.
- Think speed, and ask your employees to do the same.
- Always consider ways to offer even more convenience.

These minor weapons often provide the nudge that transforms a prospect into a customer. We all know the importance of tiny details.

Spend a few moments gaining a bit more insight into some details that probably aren't as tiny as you might think. The fact is, in the 1990s and beyond, these will be crucial components of customer service rather than details.

HOURS OF OPERATION

Many people work from nine to five. Many businesses are open those same hours. So when the people go to make a purchase, the business is closed.

Does that make sense to any red-blooded guerrilla marketer?

The nation's economy is just becoming enlightened these days to the nonsensical hours they've been open. Increasing numbers of businesses, retail and otherwise, are staying open not only until, say, eight in the evening, but for twenty-four hours a day. Amazing? Not amazing. This should have happened at the turn of the century.

Waves of guerrilla marketing enlightenment are sweeping across America. Huge supermarkets, major banks, copy shops, restaurants, and a wide variety of businesses allow you to transact business at three in the morning just as easily as you might have at three in the afternoon. Only you were working at three o'clock in the afternoon and couldn't make your purchases then.

Many catalog companies make it a simple matter to order at any hour. Not only that, but they provide you with a toll-free number and accept every credit card in the solar system. No wonder many are enjoying record-breaking profits.

Knowing that, the wise guerrilla asks, "Might my company become a catalog company? Might I put our offerings into a catalog and enable people to order any time they feel like it? Can I offer twenty-four-hour service in any possible way?"

The most prized possession of the majority of Americans is their time. You know that by now. They don't want to waste it shopping, dealing with traffic, finding a parking place, or waiting in lines.

They want to make their purchases at their convenience, not yours. They're too busy working to leave their jobs.

Who will they do business with when they are ready to buy? They are becoming aware of the growing number of businesses that are open around the clock. Do you think they'll rearrange their day to patronize an old-fashioned nine-to-five firm? Probably not. Would you?

Orient your own business to the convenience of your customers. Tell them how easy it is to purchase from you because you've expanded your hours just to make it easy.

Don't think you've got to keep doors open and people around. Although many companies must (and should) do this for their customers, it is often enough to maintain a twenty-four-hour telephone hot line for new orders, a twenty-four-hour customer service hot line, or even a fax machine that's always turned on.

DAYS OF OPERATION

A bookstore in my neck of the planet had been in business twelve years when they decided to see what happened if they started staying open on Sundays.

Being a conscientious guerrilla marketer, the owner advertised that his store would now be open seven days a week. Almost instantly, Sunday became the store's second most profitable day, following only Saturday.

Instead of being impressed with his wisdom at keeping the doors open Sunday, the owner, a guerrilla to the heart, was dismayed that he had waited twelve years to arrive at this realization.

It certainly is not difficult to see why Sunday is such a banner day for so many companies in the time-conscious society in which we now live. People want to make purchases, but they're too darned busy Mondays through Fridays, and even Saturdays.

That's why they appreciate businesses that offer the convenience of allowing purchases seven days a week. And they show their gratitude in the form of switching allegiance from their old supplier to the more convenient supplier.

Although some businesses try operating with just a skeleton force on Sundays, they frequently learn that the day is so popular with prospects and customers that a full force—sometimes even extra people—is required. As with so many other tiny-appearing, but actually humongous details of running a company, your days of operation should be directed at making yours a company with which it's easy to do business.

That probably means staying open seven days a week.

Possibly, there was a time when staying open on weekends was not a part of marketing. But today—and especially tomorrow—your days of operation are as crucial to your marketing success as your advertising and sales prowess.

It doesn't make sense to stay open more days than usual in your business unless you let people know of this. The mere fact of increased convenience is reason enough for an advertising campaign, a direct mailing, a special event, even a story in the local papers.

The times, they are a-changin'. And one of the most noticeable of these changes is the time during which business can be transacted. The more time, the greater your profits. The banks are learning that. The supermarkets are learning that. The convenience stores are learning that. Now you know that, too. If ever there's an eighth day to the week, stay open on that day.

Credit Cards Accepted

One of the objects of guerrilla marketing is to make the purchase of your offering as convenient as possible. For several crucial reasons, the acceptance of credit cards offers your customers the ultimate in convenience:

1. It enables your customers to make a purchase even if they do not have the funds at the moment.
2. It allows your customers to order by phone or mail, charging the purchase to their credit card.
3. It offers one more reason to buy: instant gratification—a powerful motivator in today's society.

Although the paperwork might be a bit easier if you accept only the two most popular credit cards, the profits will be a lot more attractive if you accept as many as you possibly can. Right now, that includes a handful.

Don't begrudge the credit cards the percentages they charge. For one thing, you'll more than make up the expense in increased profits. For another, those percentages are negotiable. See if you can arrange a lower rate.

Marketing guerrillas are proud of the purchasing convenience they offer to prospects and customers. Their marketing clearly lists the credit cards they honor.

Prospects are enticed by the symbols of the credit cards they see in store windows and on doors, in advertisements, in yellow pages ads, in brochures, in direct mailings, on postcard mailings, on coupons, and wherever the imaginative guerrilla displays them. The more places, the more profits. If you do accept credit cards, tell the world that you do. Don't keep it a secret.

If you sell a high-ticket product or service, especially one that is not normally purchased with a credit card, see if you can obtain lists of people with high limits on their credit cards. Then mail to your prospects on these lists.

Stress the fact that they can make this purchase with their credit card. That fact alone—and the pull of instant gratification—might tip the scales in your favor.

These days, you see more and more businesses willing to accept credit cards—from doctors to palm readers. If you don't yet offer your customers and prospects the ease and convenience of acting on their impulses and using a credit card to buy what you sell, I predict you'll be delighted at the upsurge in sales you'll enjoy once you accept credit cards. Stop worrying about the percentage you give the card companies. Their cards are guerrilla marketing weapons that can generate higher profits with a minimal investment.

AVAILABILITY OF FINANCING

One of the key elements in guerrilla marketing is making it convenient for your prospects to buy what you sell. An important component in offering this convenience is making it possible for your customers to pay in little chunks rather than one big hunk.

For obvious reasons, twelve easy payments of $12 each sounds a whole lot more affordable than one large payment of $130 even though the economical thing to do is pony up the $130.

Houses and automobiles were once considered the only denizens of financing land. Today, virtually anything can be financed. Items costing $25 sell more briskly if they are broken down into three handy payments. Even *Time* magazine lets you subscribe with three payments.

If financing was never available with your offering, your willingness to offer payment terms will stand you in good stead, not to mention win you the sale in most cases.

You can handle the financing arrangements yourself—for the highest profits and the most paperwork. Or you can turn the job over to a finance company or bank. This will eat into your profits but save you time filling out forms and operating the computer.

Not only should you offer financing, but you should advertise that you do. Clearly state the payments (giving people an option of three, six, nine, or twelve payments is usually best) and the actual financing terms, using accuracy and small type in your legalese.

Tell prospects the advantages of buying your offering with easy monthly payments. This may get them off the fence and onto your customer list. Perhaps you can even offer financing without charging interest. If you can do this while maintaining fiscal sanity, go for it. People love it.

Of course, you've got to be ultracareful to whom you are

offering your financing. Keep your deadbeat radar primed at all times. Ask hard questions. Demand answers that make you feel secure. Offering financing to increase profits is fine. Offering it to plunge into the red is not recommended.

In all of your marketing materials, mention that you do offer financing. This tidbit will attract business. Whether it is the kind of business you want, I don't know. But I do know that you want *some* of those prospects to become customers. It's your job to find out which ones.

Perhaps you'll offer financing on some items, but not others. That's OK, but I'm for offering it on absolutely everything so that you develop a reputation as a good company with which to do business. That's the best kind.

Catalogs

The first thing to know about catalogs is what they do not have to be: They do not have to be full-color, sixty-four pages, glossy, gorgeous, or expensively produced.

The next thing to know about catalogs is that human beings enjoy being presented with a selection, and catalogs accomplish that purpose. That is why more and more people each year purchase from catalogs.

And that is why you should consider a catalog for your company, even if catalogs are unheard of in your industry.

The idea is to offer your prospects and customers a selection. Offer them information, products, and/or services that can benefit them.

Make it extremely easy to order from your catalog. Provide a toll-free number, and accept the full gamut of credit cards. Copy your order form from the best catalogs around. The good news is that you'll be able to earn profits with your first issue. The better news is that you'll be able to gain crucial information with that same issue: which items to drop, which to emphasize, which to extend in range.

It used to be believed that you needed a customer list of 100,000 names before you should publish a catalog. It is now known that virtually any offering can be presented in catalog form and that people appreciate that form.

Catalogs show pictures. They provide information. They offer selection. They communicate the identity of the company. They make tempting offers to entice purchases, then enchanting offers to increase the size of the purchase. Catalogs are laden with marketing opportunities for guerrillas.

This is why you should find a way to use a catalog, regardless of size, colors, number of pages, and production quality. Concentrate instead on substance. Prove that yours is a catalog focusing more on straightforward customer benefits than glitzy gloss and glamour. Four pages in black and white can make a profitable catalog for your firm. While profits are never guaranteed, common sense can create them from catalogs.

Knock yourself out to present your catalog in a way that will make it stand out from the multitude of catalogs in the mailboxes of the 1990s. Your opportunity to do that is with your cover. Or your mailing envelope. Do not waste these precious opportunities to attract the attention of your readers, then lead them down the aisles of your pages.

A catalog's purpose is to generate profits by providing data that benefits readers. It can accomplish this as either a marketing weapon or a profit center or both. Worth considering.

Samples

One of the most sophisticated and successful marketing companies in the world is Procter & Gamble. Their belief in free samples is legendary.

They know that if their product is good, nothing can convey that better than a free trial of the product. So they spend a fortune giving away free samples. As a result, most of their products are the leaders in their categories.

Samples shorten the time between when a customer learns of a product or service and that same customer tries, then buys it. When you give your samples away, treat their cost—meaning, their cost to you—as a marketing investment. If your product or service offers excellence, your investment will produce excellent returns.

Consider downsizing your product or service when giving away samples. Proctor & Gamble does it with tiny tubes of toothpaste or teensy packets of laundry detergent. Guerrillas who offer services do it with abbreviated versions of their services, such as washing two windows instead of all windows, providing a free fifteen-minute consultation rather than a full hour.

I know a woman who bakes two sizes of cookies for fairs and flea markets: a tiny sample size and a large for-sale size. You can be darned sure that her tiny samples help sell a large bunch of the for-sale cookies.

You can offer free samples of both products and services. Nothing gives a prospect the experience of owning what you sell more than a free sample does. So if your product or service is shoddy, free samples will kill it in a hurry. And if it is shoddy, you should be glad for its early demise.

Make sure to give your free samples to likely prospects. Frequently, in large cities, cigarette makers offer free minipacks of cigarettes. But they ask first, "Are you a smoker?" A free sample of cigarettes in the hands of a nonsmoker makes little if any sense. So try to qualify the people to whom you will offer freebies. Be sure, if you offer free samples, that the merchandise is then readily available at local outlets. If not, you've wasted your money and your prospects' time.

Free samples have been successfully employed by manufacturers, consultants, restaurants, bakeries, food makers, cleaners, and far more. A test drive of a car is not quite a free sample, but it's as close as an auto seller can get to it. If you've been conscientious with your quality, there are few methods more effective of proving it than with a free sample, so if you can offer one, do it. If it's good enough for Proctor & Gamble, it's good enough for you.

Toll-free Phone Numbers

If you have an offering for a national audience, you certainly are easier to do business with if you have a toll-free telephone number. But if your offering is local rather than national, the toll-free part will work more against you than for you. The local phone number lets people know that you're a local person.

Should you decide to have a toll-free service, I suggest that you first attend one of your local telephone company's or AT&T's telemarketing seminars. You'll learn there are several ways to offer toll-free phone service.

The hardest and most effective way, at least at first, is to install your own 800 number and either answer it yourself or have a well-trained employee do the same. By keeping it in-house, you'll have better control, be more in touch with reality, be able to talk to prospects and learn their questions, and be positioned to work out any bugs.

Some of my clients find so much security in this that they have several employees handling incoming calls—an entire department—and they find it worth the cost.

Another way to offer toll-free convenience is to hire an 800 answering service. Find them in your business directory or yellow pages under "Telemarketing Research and Selling Services." Quite a few are listed, and guess what? It doesn't cost you a penny to call them. Most are toll-free.

They can accept phone calls to you, give information, make a sales pitch, answer simple questions, and take orders and shipping information. Naturally, you'll have to find the ones that do the job best—but AT&T can give you some good hints. Select with care. A good service makes a big difference.

Another option is a telephone-answering device that attaches to a computer and takes and/or gives data. These days, people don't mind the impersonality of answering devices as much as they used to. What they do mind is an inability to get in touch with you.

So your toll-free 800 number, especially one that operates seven days a week, twenty-four hours a day, will make them happy.

Face up to the fact that some people hate to talk on the phone. These people write for information or to place orders. Other people hate to write. These people need a toll-free number or you'll never hear from them. If you do install such a number, and you plan to advertise it on radio or TV, be sure you make it something like 800-748-6444 instead of a wordy number like 800-CALLJIM. People will write down the number. They'll entrust the words to their memory, then forget them the next day. Don't say I didn't warn you.

CREDIBILITY

Prospects won't buy what you sell if you don't have credibility. You know how important confidence is. To earn it, you've got to be aware of your "metamessage"—the unstated, yet powerful communication in your marketing materials. It's the look and feel of your marketing.

You can begin your quest for credibility with guerrilla marketing weapons such as your name, your logo, your theme line, your location, and your interior decor. Gain more credibility with your stationery, business card, package, brochure, business forms, employee attire, and advertising—both what your advertising says and where it appears.

Increase your credibility with professional telephone demeanor, neatness throughout your operation, caring service, regular follow-up, and community involvement. Testimonials add to your credibility. So do professional affiliations. And so do satisfied customers—especially the kind who will gladly talk up your business.

Word-of-mouth is heavy artillery in the battle for credibility. Want a few shortcuts to credibility? The answer should be a resounding "Yes!" OK, here are a few: write that article or column for a publication, publish a book, give a seminar, make a speech, get a publicity story in the newspaper or get invited onto a radio or TV talk show, then deport yourself in a way to gain credibility.

One of the easiest paths to credibility is a full-page ad in a regional edition of a respected national magazine. The ad won't net you much credibility, but the reprints you display, mail, incorporate into your other marketing, and proudly disseminate, will. Count on it.

You can gain major-league credibility with a professional PR effort. Be sure to make reprints of the publicity stories. Frame them. Make them part of your brochure.

The most certain avenue to credibility, along with quality

and service, is not a shortcut, but a longcut. It is commitment to a marketing program, then consistent execution of it—week in, week out, month in, month out, year after year after year. By doing this, you are proving your credibility beyond the power of mere words.

People equate consistent marketing with credibility. Even people who have never met you will believe in you and have confidence in you if they ever need you. See? Even with credibility you have to convince folks that they need you.

It's interesting to note how much credibility you can gain without advertising. Advertising is a big help, but the real credibility will come over time—if you have the quality to back it up.

SATISFIED CUSTOMERS

When compiling the list of 100 guerrilla marketing weapons, I often wondered which was best. This is it. The best not only costs you no money, but it earns money for you. There are few if any other marketing weapons with the power, cost-effectiveness, and economy of satisfied customers.

Here are the main reasons they are so valuable:

1. They have a wonderful way of being transformed into repeat customers.
2. They have a delightful manner of obtaining referral customers for you.

Naturally, these two blessings do not occur automatically. You've got to earn them. Earn the repeat business of customers by providing a product, service, or store that is so good that they want more of what you're selling. Earn referral business by providing quality with value and by controlling the word-of-mouth advertising that pays off on your bottom line.

Gain this control by providing brochures to your satisfied customers, thereby putting the words into their mouths. Gain it by writing to satisfied customers—even asking them to refer customers to you. You might even "bribe" them with a gift or a discount in return for each new customer who mentions their name. Yes, you'll get the word-of-mouth marketing if you're good enough. But you'll gain more of it, and faster, if you ask for it.

Savvy marketers spend 10 percent of their marketing budgets talking to the universe in general; they spend 30 percent talking to prospects; they spend 60 percent of it talking to satisfied customers. If you spend 60 percent talking to your own satisfied customers, that does not represent a lot of money—especially when compared with standard mass-media marketing. So keep a list of those satisfied customers and keep marketing to them, reminding them of past satisfaction and offering future satisfaction.

If you consider every single satisfied customer to be an unofficial member of your sales force, you've got the right idea. Only, unlike salespeople who only sell your offering, satisfied customers sell *and buy* your offering, a winning combination if ever there was one. And always remember that it costs only one-fifth as much to keep an old customer as it does to earn a new one.

So treat your satisfied customers with love, loyalty, devotion, consideration, and professionalism. That, plus their positive experience with you, will keep them satisfied. The more satisfied customers you have, the more satisfied customers you'll gain. It's an endless circle that gets bigger and bigger—along with your profits. And that's just what a guerrilla wants—and deserves.

7
WEAPONS THAT ARE FREQUENTLY MISUSED

If you pick up a hand grenade, pull the pin, and forget to throw it, you've got major trouble coming soon. So it goes with guerrilla marketing weapons, too.

A company decides it should put together a brochure to herald its glories to the world, then creates something so ill-advised that each person who sees it gets turned off to the company. Perhaps the brochure is loaded with exaggerations. Possibly it has misspelled words and poor English. And then it may be overly technical. Maybe it whets the reader's appetite but withholds the important details that will help that reader decide to buy.

And there's always the chance that it inadvertently offends somebody. Many old assumptions about life and people are no longer universally accepted. Stay clear of any sensitive issues.

Have you ever heard of negative marketing? If not, I'm certain you've been exposed to it. Negative marketing is the improper use of marketing—so improper that it actually loses more sales than it gains. If fifty people decide to buy the product as a result of the marketing, and seventy more decide to quit using it or stay away from it forever, that's negative marketing.

Negative marketing often occurs when a nonguerrilla employs a weapon in an amateurish fashion. The person may only be trying to save money—in fact, that's usually the case. But the net result is negativity about the product or service.

You can avoid negative marketing if you use only weapons that you can use properly. If you don't know how to use them properly yourself, find someone who can. The earth is not teeming with these people, but there are a lot of them around. Just because you don't know how to create a telemarketing script doesn't mean you shouldn't profit by telemarketing. Instead, find an expert to create the script for you. You don't need an advertising agency. In fact, most agencies would be confused if asked to create a telemarketing script. It would probably come out sounding like a radio commercial.

There are three main reasons to avoid misusing a marketing weapon:

1. Misusing weapons results in negative marketing.
2. Misusing weapons is a waste of your money.
3. Misusing weapons undermines your credibility.

I could probably come up with five more reasons to treat guerrilla marketing weapons with care, but I have the feeling that these three will suffice for you.

Misusing a weapon is hardly in the spirit of guerrilla marketing. That's why this chapter is here: to protect you against wasting your money and your time. The 8 weapons covered here are not the only weapons that are misused, but in my experience they are misused the most. If I were to add one more weapon to this chapter, it would be television, but we'll look into its use—and abuse—in Chapter 9.

The awful actuality is that all 100 marketing weapons can be misused and are misused every day. But I selected those that seem to attract the hordes. Hope you're not one of them.

Some of the marketing truths set forth in this chapter will never be learned by your competitors, and isn't that a break for you? Not only will they never misuse a telemarketing script, they won't develop one in the first place.

Outside signs are the first weapons covered here. The colors, typefaces, copy, and location make these quite easy to misuse. I don't want you following in the footsteps of the vast army of misusers.

Word-of-mouth marketing will be explored next. It is not, regardless of the depth of your faith, in the hands of a Higher Power. Instead, it is smack-dab in your mortal hands. So don't fail to capitalize on it. Prayer is powerful in many situations. It is a waste of your zeal when it comes to getting word-of-mouth referrals.

Brochures are the darlings of guerrillas because they enable them to convey so much important data. But brochures are the bane of a nonguerrilla's existence: expensive, ineffective, and frequently in need of revision.

Yellow pages ads cost a lot of money, so if you misuse them, they waste a lot of money. And scads of companies misuse them. When you complete this chapter, I'm sure that list won't include your company.

Public relations are high-impact, instant-result, marvelous credibility weapons—but only for those who understand the truth about PR. The truth is not, sadly, what most of small business America knows. But this truth is, happily, coming up in just a few pages. Knowing it will save you from grief, false expectations, poor timing, and an unrealistic marketing plan. A good plan does include public relations, the kind that really and truly does result in free publicity for your firm, not the kind that involves sending a blizzard of press releases and seeing naught in return.

Telemarketing scripts are misused primarily because they

are not used. There's no excuse for not using them if you're a guerrilla. Ask any guerrilla.

Co-operative advertising funds by the billion (really!) are available for entrepreneurs to use, but these stanchions of capitalism haven't a clue as to how to access those funds. By the end of the chapter, they'll know. And so will you.

As long as you're going to have access to co-op funds, why not take advantage of co-op marketing materials, expensively produced ads and brochures that are yours for the asking? Why not, indeed? Because small business owners are lost in the woods when it comes to getting their hands on these materials and saving the money they represent. Again, they are misused because they are not used. I'll put an end to that. Just wait and see.

My goal is for you to use as many guerrilla marketing weapons as you can use properly. If the weapon is not producing a profit for you, it is not being used properly. The idea is to maximize your profits, and you'll do that only if you use the weapons of guerrilla marketing with skill and intelligence.

Some of the weapons in this chapter don't cost a cent, in the true spirit of guerrilla marketing. But even those, if improperly employed, can waste your time and energy. These are precious commodities, and must not be squandered through misuse. Guerrillas waste nothing—not money, not time, and not energy. At least that's what it says here.

Outside Signs

Outside signs help you gain awareness, tie in with your other marketing, promote your business away from your business location, and capitalize on impulse reactions.

Signs may be displayed outside on billboards, buildings, bulletin boards, benches, barns, buses, wind shelters, taxis, and in the businesses of others. In fact, the potential locations for signs are limited only by your imagination. Use it; you'll come up with more locations.

The rule of thumb about signs is that they should tell your story as visually as possible, and they should contain a maximum of six words. That rule is especially applicable to signs that will be viewed by passing motorists.

If other than motorists will read your signs, you can add to that six-word maximum. But six is the maximum comfortably taken in at a single glance.

Ideally, your signs will have the same theme, same offer, or same benefits that you are marketing in other media. If so, those other media will work better. So will the signs.

It is crucial to use an ultraclear typeface on your signs, and to be sure that the words are clearly readable against the color background you select. If you are going to use signs, it's a good idea to visit a sign company or two to learn the state-of-the-sign art.

Because of the ability of signs to generate impulse reactions you should tell people how to locate your business if it is nearby. Phrases that do this successfully are "next exit," "two miles," "next right turn," and things of that ilk. If you can use them, do so. You'll be gratified at the reaction. Impulses are very important motivators.

Be sure your sign is clean. If it isn't, people will assume you run a sloppy business. Be sure it is different enough from other signs so as not to confuse your prospects. If you can, use a series of signs—such as Burma-Shave did.

Harold's Club in Reno became famous with signs placed throughout the United States. Same for Wall Drugs in South Dakota.

Those businesses were able to prosper using signs and no other marketing weapons. But they are rare. Usually, signs cannot do the selling job all by themselves.

Look around your community for bulletin boards; they're ideal for signs. My own community has six hundred such bulletin boards. Some advertisers blow up their ads to use as signs.

When you consider the multitude of locations visited or passed by your prospects, you'll appreciate the economy and the cohesiveness that outdoor signs can offer your business.

WORD-OF-MOUTH

Very few companies can prosper using only word-of-mouth marketing. Fewer still can be launched with so capricious a marketing medium. It is possible to earn profits without advertising—but advertising is only one of the 100 marketing weapons. Many other weapons should be used.

Word-of-mouth will become perhaps the most effective of those weapons if you provide consistent quality, top-level service, conscientious follow-up, and an unblemished reputation.

The longer your customer list, the more possibilities you have for word-of-mouth referrals. You can do several things to increase your word-of-mouth marketing so that as little as possible is left to chance. Consider these options:

1. Create brochures to be given to customers only, and solely at the time of purchase. People are most apt to talk up a new purchase within the first thirty days after they make it. This way, you put the right words in the right mouths at the right time. Give those brochures to nobody else.
2. Write a letter to customers asking them to talk up your company—if they were happy with the product or service purchased. Tell them you'll send them a free gift for any customer who mentions their name. Works surprisingly well.
3. Learn who your customers patronize, then prove your quality to them. Example: A new restaurant opened and gave coupons good for two free dinners to all the hair salon owners within a one-mile radius of the restaurant. The quality was great; no strings were attached to the offer; the word-of-mouth was instant and extremely gratifying. See how you can apply this concept to your business.

4. Prove your expertise with free offerings in the form of seminars, newspaper or magazine articles, lectures, a local column, appearing on local radio talk shows, and/or newsletters. Word-of-mouth will be favorable even from people who have not yet been your customers—but probably will be soon.

Favorable word-of-mouth spreads slowly—unless you do something about it.

Unfavorable word-of-mouth spreads like wildfire. One person is responsible for twenty-two other people hearing about the bad experience. And that's just the average. The big mouths tell even more people.

The most successful guerrilla companies gain word-of-mouth marketing only after several years of aggressive marketing on the other battlefields: advertising, direct marketing, sampling, demonstrations, and the dedication to amassing an army of satisfied customers. Only then can they cut back on their marketing budgets and watch the referral business flow in.

Brochures

Brochures have several advantages over most of the other marketing vehicles available to you. Probably the most important advantage is that brochures can convey a lot of information about your business. Some people have the notion that brochures should have short copy. In some cases that may be true.

But in most cases, the more you tell the more you'll sell. People don't read brochures unless they are seriously interested in gaining data. They are not interested in "white space"; they are interested in learning more about your business. And they resent it if you don't give them enough information to make a decision about what you are selling.

So use visuals: photos, illustrations, sketches, charts, graphs, diagrams, whatever. But don't deny your prospects the written data that will create in them a desire to buy.

A delightful aspect of brochures is that they enable you to save a bundle on your advertising while creating a separate source of cash flow. They do this by allowing you to run tiny ads in several publications, each ad communicating the single prime benefit of doing business with you. The ads then invite prospects to call or write for a free brochure. Via this method, you can disseminate many reasons to purchase from you without paying for the advertising space to do so. That's how you save on advertising.

Add the names of the brochure-requesters to your mailing list and write to them regularly. Rent their names, once you have at least a thousand, to list brokers who will pay you for the privilege of reaching people with an identified interest. That's how they improve your cash flow.

Here are some valuable suggestions for guerrillas with an eye toward adding brochures to their marketing arsenals:

1. Consider using three-fold (six-panel) brochures that neatly fit into a #10 envelope, a pocket, or a file.

2. Spare the expense of color, unless you really need it. Use the space to convey information. Do it in an aesthetically pleasing way but don't indulge in unnecessary expenses.
3. Consider using a larger brochure with a flap inside the rear cover to hold 8½-by-11-inch sheets of paper that further your cause and home in on specific targets.
4. Create brochures that may be used for years. Instead of writing "We're ten years old," write "We were founded in 1981."
5. Spread the word with brochures through ads, through customers, and through outlets where your prospects may pick them up. The more places you use them, the more you'll love brochures.

Yellow Pages Ads

There are an increasing number of telephone directories. If you can, use the largest while testing another. You might end up in several directories. Never mind the cost. If it's small compared with the sales attributed to your proper yellow pages marketing, you won't mind its size.

The yellow pages give you an opportunity to go head-to-head with your competition. You can promote your business with the same size ad as your largest competitor, and even if your business is new, you can appear as well established as your oldest competitor. Here are three fundamental truths about marketing via the yellow pages:

1. If other businesses in your industry aren't listing themselves or running ads, perhaps it means the people in your market don't look for businesses such as yours in the yellow pages. Consider not listing or listing inexpensively.
2. The people who seek out your ad in the yellow pages are honest prospects for what you sell. They are not browsing the yellow pages. So devote no space toward flagging their attention. You've already got it.
3. Be sure your yellow pages ad provides loads of information. Don't waste valuable space as "white space" or in showing unnecessary pictures. Give all the benefits of dealing with your business. Tell a lot; sell a lot.

In most cases, the color red pays for itself in the yellow pages. A few years from now, when more people discover that little gem, it may not be true anymore. But it is now. Soon, many other colors will be available besides red.

If you do get a lot of calls from your yellow pages ad, be absolutely certain that the people answering your telephone are trained to maintain the sales momentum and convert the inquirer into a buyer. That requires that they know your yellow pages ad by heart.

When you must decide: (1) In which sections do I advertise? and (2) In which editions do I advertise? the answers are to be found (1) by asking others in your field who are located in a noncompetitive area, and (2) by experimenting with smaller ads at first. Source every caller.

People consult the yellow pages intentionally. If you sell computers and you ask "Looking for a Computer?" in your headline, the readers' answer will always be yes, enabling you to take advantage of an existing interest in buying. Word of advice: Don't let the yellow pages people write or design your ad. Give that job to a professional. It's well worth the cost. And ask your yellow pages rep about the new electronic yellow pages that lists a phone number, which allows you to amplify upon and change your phone message monthly.

If you employ radio or TV advertising, *never* tell people to find your number in the yellow pages. They'll discover all of your competitors and rarely get to you. List in the yellow pages, but direct people to the *white* pages.

PUBLIC RELATIONS

There are two wonderful things and two terrible things about public relations. Let's start with the wonderful:

1. PR gives you loads of credibility.
2. PR doesn't cost you a dime.

Then, let's move on to the terrible:

1. You cannot repeat PR as you can ads.
2. You have no control over PR. *No say-so whatsoever.*

Although news you generate about your business may be read in the daily paper, heard on the radio, and seen on television, the cost for that publicity, sometimes to millions of people, can be as low as zero. On the other hand, if you hire a PR pro, it could run a few thousand per month.

It is possible to generate your own PR. Here's how: Do or create something newsy for the media. They want fascinating news as much as you want free exposure. Provide that news, along with a publicity release story, a fact sheet, and a black-and-white glossy photo, to the appropriate people at the appropriate media. Find out who they are from your reference librarian or hire a pro. Keep writing, phoning, even showing up. Invite them to dinner. To breakfast. PR pros are on a first-name basis with these folks.

They know that the secret is, after good solid news, the right contacts along with enough determination. They've got both. If you don't, hire a PR pro. You won't be sorry.

If printed publicity appears, make reprints of it and mail it all over the place. Blow it up, frame it, and put it where the maximum number of your prospects can see it. Turn it into a mailing piece. Milk it or it will dry out on its own. A cardinal guerrilla sin is failure to reprint publicity.

Public relations consists not only of media coverage of your business but of all the relations you have with the public. This can include special events, turkey races, parade floats, contests, races, film festivals, essay contests, bakeoffs; the list is limited only by the expanse of your imagination.

Sponsorship of teams and joining of local clubs also falls into the category of public relations. The two biggest mistakes you can make in PR are (1) having publicity appear prematurely—before you're ready to sell—and (2) thinking that a powerful PR effort is all it takes to succeed at marketing.

The real skinny about PR is that without a publicity contact of your own, or a slew of them, you've got only a tiny chance of garnering the free publicity you seek. The way of the PR world is that, if you've got a contact, you'll get the coverage.

TELEMARKETING SCRIPTS

There are two distinct views about the use of telemarketing scripts as marketing devices. First, understand that telemarketing works unquestionably better with the use of such scripts.

The first camp argues that scripts should be *idea scripts*, comprised of a few verbatim opening lines, a list of ideas to cover, and a few verbatim closing lines. Advocates of idea scripts say this offers the caller more flexibility. The second camp suggests that you use *verbatim scripts*, with every word spelled out. Proponents of verbatim scripts say this ensures that each caller will use proven words and phrases to make a sale and that flexibility in telemarketing is more of a vice than a virtue. As a guerrilla, I agree.

Verbatim scripts should be so well memorized that they don't sound memorized at all. Callers should learn them by listening to tapes of successful telemarketers so that callers can learn the phrases as well as the phrasing and intonations. The right words with the wrong voice inflections don't close sales.

This is the hardest type of telemarketing script to perfect, but also the most effective. Idea scripts are far easier to work with—from the standpoint of a caller and a company. They require no specific voice inflection and no memorization. It helps, though, if a few "magic" phrases, proven in real life, are included for the benefit of the caller . . . and the company.

The best telemarketing scripts come on the heels of a direct mailing—increasing the mail response rate by anywhere from 6 percent to 22 percent. These idea scripts start with a few questions designed to elicit yes answers. One of the questions might be a totally nonbusiness question to help establish a human bond. After the opening questions, the caller asks questions centered on the offering. These questions are usually preceded by sales points about features and benefits, taking five to fifteen seconds each.

At the conclusion, which might be as short as one minute, or as long as five minutes after the start of the call, the caller closes by asking for the order or for the person being called to take the next step required, such as answering specific questions relating to the order.

The purpose of any telemarketing script is to advance the sale. This is why telemarketing expenditures surpassed those of direct mail way back in 1982. The key to a good script is to develop rapport, so be sure your telemarketing scripts, whichever type, have a feel of warmth and humanity. Get this feel by having callers frequently use the prospect's name. OK? Gotta hang up now.

ACCESS TO CO-OP FUNDS

Many manufacturers want you to mention their name in your marketing. To motivate you to do this, they make large sums of money available, called co-op funds—which is short for cooperative advertising funds.

In most cases, you must mention the name of the manufacturer, show their logo, perhaps quote their theme line, then fill out a form and enclose reprints of your ads or scripts of your radio or TV commercials, duly noted by the station.

In return for going through these steps, the manufacturer will send you a check. If you are conscientious enough about going after your co-op funds, they can handle up to about half of your marketing budget.

But the paperwork is usually so complex that advertisers are put off by it, so they skip this unique opportunity. In fact, in 1989, a full $2.5 *billion* in co-op funds went unclaimed because advertisers did not know how to gain access to them.

Because I want no guerrilla to lose out on the opportunity to obtain co-op funds, I implore you to ask any manufacturer from whom you buy about their co-op program. If they have none, suggest that they institute one. After all, you're willing to share in the cost of mentioning their name in your marketing and advertising.

Whatever you do, get the free information about accessing co-op funds by contacting Benard and Company. Call them at 415-957-5886 and ask for their free brochure. That could be the most profitable call you'll ever make.

I also suggest that you look into the pure concept of co-op marketing—especially if you don't do business with companies that make the funds available. Perhaps you can share the cost of marketing and advertising with companies that are compatible with yours—such as a tile retailer if you're a tile installer, or vice versa.

If you are able to access co-op funds, you'll find it worth the initial hassle and paperwork. Mentioning the name of a big-time company, probably a national advertiser itself, will add to your own credibility and not hurt your own advertising one bit.

By availing yourself of all the co-op funds to which you're entitled, you can cut the cost of your marketing while increasing its effectiveness, a guerrillalike maneuver if ever there was one. Some of my clients have half their ad budgets paid by co-op funds. Sure it took time to get those funds. But ask the clients if it was worth the effort.

Is any of that $2.5 billion yours? I hope you find out!

ACCESS TO MARKETING MATERIALS

Companies seem to make one of two common errors in the production of their marketing materials: either they overspend on glitz and frills or they spend too little, conveying the identity of a shoddy and unprofessional business. Both are wasting precious money.

Of all the methods of communicating with professional, intelligent, well-conceived, and often brilliant marketing materials, the least expensive is the obtaining of the marketing vehicle materials you'll need at little or no cost.

Many large companies, both manufacturing and service, give small businesses access to professionally (and lavishly) produced marketing materials absolutely free. Others charge a teeny-weeny, nominal fee for them. The marketing and advertising materials to which they give ready access include:

- Brochures
- Magazine ad slicks
- Newspaper ad slicks
- Catalogs and catalog sheets
- Premium gifts
- Newsletters
- TV commercial tapes
- Radio commercial tapes
- Signs of all types
- Music for marketing needs
- Show display materials
- Direct-mail components

It would cost you a fortune to produce all those goodies. But if your business deals with companies that provide them, you can have theirs for free—or for a pittance. Just ask.

All of the marketing materials to which you may have access can be imprinted with your name, logo, theme, address, phone, and in many cases, with your own special message. It's your guerrilla marketing, but someone else paid for it.

Check with your suppliers to see if they provide marketing materials for their customers. If you spend money marketing, you can save gobs of it by utilizing these weapons. After all, they were created specifically for you. That leaves you free to invest in media and mailing instead of production.

In many cases, the same companies that grant access to advertising materials also make advertising co-op funds available to their customers. Be sure to ask about it.

Although you can save a bundle by capitalizing on your free access to first-rate marketing materials, don't do it if you feel you must compromise your company's individuality. Perhaps the materials are at odds with your own marketing. Either adapt them to your needs or ignore them.

If you're buying something to sell to others, don't ignore the possibility that the company from which you are buying may be investing in marketing materials that you can use. If they're not, perhaps they should. It's definitely worth asking about. Guerrillas are famed for being squeaky wheels.

8

WEAPONS THAT PRODUCE INSTANT RESULTS

The man asked the pet store owner why one particular parrot was priced at $5,000. "Because he can sing 'Deck the Halls,' " explained the proprietor.

"I'll pay you five thousand dollars if the bird can sing that song," said the skeptical shopper. Without a moment's hesitation, the bird burst into song, filling the pet shop with a hearty rendition of the classic Christmas carol.

The man wrote a check for $5,000, took the bird home, and amused himself each evening by requesting the tune. A few weeks later, the man had a big Christmas Eve party at his house. While the parrot was being admired, the man announced to his guests that the bird could sing "Deck the Halls." Many of the guests doubted it and a bet was taken up, the host betting $5,000 that the bird could sing the song in its entirety.

"Sing the song," the man smilingly requested of his parrot. But there was absolute silence. "Sing 'Deck the Halls,' " said the man, a bit louder. Still nothing; not a sound to be heard. "Sing it! The song!" implored the man. Again, cold, unbroken silence.

Forlornly, the man paid the $5,000 to his betting guests, who soon left. When everyone was gone, he faced the silent parrot. "Why didn't you sing that song?" the man demanded.

"Dumbhead!" shot back the parrot. "Think of the odds you'll get with 'Auld Lang Syne' next week!"

Many of the weapons that produce the instant gratification business owners seek are often employed at less than 100 percent effectiveness because they're used too soon or too often, or too much to the exclusion of other weapons.

Often, the weapon is underpowered because the timing is wrong. The parrot knew that. The profits would be far higher if they waited just one week. Although these weapons can and do produce money in a hurry, the key to succeeding with many of them is restraint.

Guerrilla marketing is not oriented to devoting your efforts toward obtaining instant results. Guerrilla marketing focuses your attention on the long-term view, on staying in business, growing, and prospering for as long as you want. Quick-fix marketing denies you those freedoms. Guerrilla marketing does have quick results inherent within it. Some times you absolutely need a healthy injection of cash into the flow. But you've got to balance that with healthy injections of customer bonding. Guerrillas want both: money *and* lasting customer relationships.

All 16 of the following instant income weapons have been used by businesses, large and small, to generate sales and profits—*snap!*—that quick.

Because of the nature of your business, you won't be able to stock your arsenal with all 16 of these, but you will be able to find a way to use some of them, and just 1 or 2 can bring a smile to your banker's face. Because with every page and every word you are becoming more and more of a guerrilla. I know you'll realize the need to experiment, to try as many of these as you possibly can, eliminating the time-wasters, concentrating on the cash-attracters.

Some of these seem tiny and insignificant when viewed on their own. Doorhangers, for example, hardly seem like a way to bring home the bacon in a hurry. But when a spectacular offer is made on them, requiring a phone call by the homeowner, and that call results in a sales presentation that becomes a bona fide sale with a world-class profit, the doorhanger is no longer tiny.

The connection from the prospect's wallet to your deposit slip is like a long steel chain. Few of the weapons can reach the whole distance. But when they combine as links, the chain reaches. A doorhanger is a link. Small, but made of tempered steel.

Inside signs are the first of the weapons we'll investigate. Because they generate impulse sales, "instant results" is what interior signage can accomplish.

Although preparing for a trade show takes months, the results trade-show displays produce occur in a flash, with one flash after another at the trade show—if you go about your trade show marketing properly.

Fairs and flea markets don't require a whole lot of waiting around. You make the sale or you don't. Even if you make only one sale for every hundred people who see your booth, if ten thousand people show up, you'll be making many sales.

Special events can be used to generate publicity, goodwill, or instant sales. Sometimes you can obtain all those good things. With a bit of imagination, or a resourceful PR person, the possibilities for special events are unlimited.

Searchlights and blimps are turning out to be companions of special events because they call attention to them, serving as links in the chain, albeit one link filled with helium.

Seminars and workshops can bestow instant authority on you—or instant money, depending on how you set them up. Courses and lectures were examined as instant credibility builders in Chapter 5. So we'll view seminars and workshops as instant profit builders here in Chapter 8.

Effective displays can move merchandise, in the blink

of an eye, from the display to the customer's hands. Such displays must be included in any chapter that looks into guerrilla marketing weapons that produce instant results.

Demonstrations are famous for the speed at which they get the prospect's name on the dotted line. The vacuum cleaner salesperson spills the dirt on the carpet, then vacuums it up, demonstrating the cleaner and making the sale. Well, it's not always that easy. On second thought, for some guerrillas, it is.

Consultations are a method of demonstration in that they enable you to demonstrate your wisdom, or better yet, your ability to solve problems, or perhaps even produce instant results. What we have here is a weapon that can produce instant results because it shows others how to obtain instant results.

Sales presentations are designed solely to result in a sale. After all, there's the opening contact, then the sales presentation, and finally, the close. Many people know that sales presentations are supposed to bring about instant results. They just don't know how to do them. To the rescue, Chapter 8.

Direct-mail letters are weapons that you keep stockpiled so you can have them ready rather than develop them after you discover you need them. Either way, if they're part of a more comprehensive marketing effort, they can bring in the cash in a great big hurry.

Direct-mail postcards can do the very same thing with less of an investment, take less time to create, and offer more of a chance that the recipient will read your offer.

Postcard deck offers are coupons masquerading as postcards joined up with many other masquerading postcards encased in a plastic wrap. Of the 100 guerrilla marketing weapons, this is probably the fastest-growing.

Booths for malls are also increasing in popularity because malls are proliferating, as is awareness of the need to market like a guerrilla. A booth is the perfect opportunity. A mall is the perfect place.

Doorhangers don't just hang on doorknobs. They entice a person to make a call, buy a product, visit a store, or send for more information. Alone, they're just dinky little pieces of cardboard or paper. As part of a team, they can be devastating.

Sales representatives are geared and poised for instant results. They know it takes a multitude of sales calls to close many sales. But they want that sale right this very moment if they're worth their salt. And so they try to make it. Still, I'd be remiss if I didn't warn you that this sixteenth weapon doesn't always produce instant results. But it can, it has, and it might for you.

Some of the 16 weapons about to be scrutinized produce profits faster than others. None ask that you wait as long as, say, a television campaign. Even McDonald's, with their lavish production and brilliant commercials, doesn't really expect you to rush out and buy a Big Mac the moment after you've seen their spot.

It must be enticing to consider which of these weapons will be most appropriate for adding an upward thrust to your sales curve. It is enticing, but it can be dangerous.

Don't put all your marketing efforts into the instant result arena or smart competitors will steal your customers by employing maneuvers that breed more loyalty. Instead, incorporate a variety of these weapons into your complete marketing recipe—aiming for a healthy balance of short-term gain and long-term survival.

Guerrillas should always incorporate balance in marketing.

Inside Signs

Each year, it becomes more apparent that signs inside trigger impulse reactions that are manifested in sales. In 1989, nearly 70 percent of all purchases were made by inside signs, if we're to believe the Point-of-Purchase Advertising Institute in Chicago. They also tell us that in that same year over $7 billion was spent on inside signs—indicating the popularity of signs among the big spenders.

Inside signs allow you to merchandise the items for which the customers entered your place of business in the first place, then cross-merchandise those offerings they may not have known were available.

Sophisticated guerrillas with large showrooms and sparse sales forces treat their signs as silent salespeople. Just as national parks have self-guiding nature trails with signs that tell you what you're seeing from the path, these showrooms have self-guiding sales trails with signs that sell you what you're seeing in the showroom.

By the time a customer encounters a salesperson, the sale is nearly made. The signs have done all the hard work. And you can be sure they've left out nary a detail. Do people mind reading long copy on interior signs? Of course not. People enter a selling establishment with buying on their minds. They have a fairly clear notion of what they'll purchase, but their minds are open. Signs do a whale of a job penetrating, informing, and enticing those open minds.

Keep your signs within the bounds of your own identity. If your ads are great-looking and your products first-rate, garish signs won't help your case. Perhaps you'll want to frame your signs. Some might hang on a wall. Others may be freestanding. It depends on the convenience of the customers.

Other than the standard ideas for signs, such as item and price, consider nonstandard ideas, such as framed reprints of your magazine ad, a blowup of your newspaper ad, your brochure (showing both sides), framed testimonial letters (extremely potent; extremely inexpensive), framed publicity stories, and anything else you might recognize as signworthy.

Aside from your own store, consider inside signs in the stores of others (on a cooperative basis), inside buses, inside taxis, inside subway cars, in windows (yours and the windows of others), and anywhere else your target audience may appear in large numbers.

Use inside signs that are not in your location as forums for a lot of information about your business. Short copy should not be used unless you have a highly tempting offer. People have time inside. They'll use it to read. For a good feeling deep inside, add inside signs to your marketing mix.

Trade Show Displays

Although I implore all would-be guerrillas to use a large assortment of the 100 guerrilla marketing weapons at their disposal, I must admit that some of my clients get all the business—and profits—they need at trade shows.

They do it with a dynamic trade show display and a deep understanding of the purpose of most trade shows. That purpose is to close sales. There's another purpose, too: to obtain names for a mailing list. And there's a third purpose as well: to make contacts and intensify relationships.

The companies that do the worst at trade shows focus on a fourth purpose, which is really only a fringe benefit: the chance to display merchandise. Displaying goods, especially new things, is laudable, but it is not the reason for most trade shows.

Most trade shows are loaded with intelligent sellers interested in selling a year's worth of goods to each show attendee and with buyers interested in making a sage purchase of a year's worth. If the boothholder isn't oriented to serious selling, the buyer will be frustrated and the seller will be losing out on potential sales and profits. For this reason, it makes sense to do at least these five things for each trade show at which you have a display:

1. Distribute circulars directing people to your display by handing them out at the entrance or by slipping them under the doors of rooms at nearby hotels where attendees are staying.
2. Have a sweepstakes that people can enter simply by dropping their business cards into a bowl. This nets you a lot of names for your all-important prospect mailing list. Write to these people within thirty days of the show. It also brings these people to your booth. even if only to drop off their business cards to enter your sweepstakes.

3. Have a "closing area" in your booth—table, chairs, order form, privacy—where sales may be closed on the spot.
4. Be sure at least four people run your booth. You'll need them to relieve each other. Standing on your feet selling all day is very taxing. You need rest and relief to be at your best.
5. Have a hospitality suite in a nearby hotel where your best customers and prospects can be given the royal treatment that they deserve. This is where relationships are solidified.

Your trade show display should appeal to both right- and left-brained people: that is, it should have emotional, aesthetic appeal with many gorgeous graphic elements, as well as logical, sequential reasoning with words that make sense and win sales. Do all you can to demonstrate your offering. If that's not feasible, use videotape or slide technology to show what you are selling. Remember that points made to the eye are far more effective than points made to the ear alone. And keep in mind that people who attend trade shows are in a buying mood. So be sure that you and your cohorts are in a selling mood.

If you're going to attend a trade show, along with remembering about that buying mood, there are five things you want to know:

1. Know what you want to accomplish.
2. See the entire show; profits hide in esoteric places.
3. Prioritize by visiting the important exhibits first.
4. Bring a sturdy, lightweight case to hold show materials.
5. Wear comfortable shoes; take breaks to lighten your load.

If you're an exhibitor, all you've really got to focus on is getting your prospect's attention and time, then showing how you can help the prospect profit.

Fairs and Flea Markets

Many successful guerrillas do all of their marketing only at fairs and flea markets. Some of them need only four successful fairs to earn a year's worth of income. Others work a flea market every single weekend of the year.

While you may not do all of your marketing at these large public gatherings—which include swap meets, open markets, farmers' markets, crafts fairs, expos, Renaissance Faires, and all other such forms of mass commerce—you should open your mind to the possibilities they might mean for your company.

Perhaps you should rent booth space to display the benefits of your product or service while selling it with verve. Please recognize that services can be successfully merchandised at these venues just as handily as products.

If you can't see the profit in your own booth, consider sharing space with some compatible entrepreneur, one whose offering complements yours, and/or vice versa. For you, the entrepreneur represents a new point of distribution and a sales rep. For the entrepreneur, you represent a new source of profits. At least that should be the goal of any booth sharing.

Guerrillas market at fairs and markets with the idea of selling their offerings, not merely exhibiting them. They accomplish this noble goal by having an attention-getting visual element to capture the fancy of passersby. Such elements include signs, mannequins, mimes, balloons, helium-filled inflatables, and imaginatively showcased products. Be wise; you'll be competing with wise marketers.

Once the attention of prospects has been attracted, signs and fascinating displays should entice them even deeper. The signs should give substantial reasons—both emotional and intellectual—why the person should buy right now.

Fairs and markets have two delightfully unique features that work in your favor:

1. Most of the people attending are in the mood to buy and expect to make purchases. There is often a buying frenzy.
2. You can offer potential customers the delirious glee of instant gratification because your offering is right there, all set to be possessed by a customer. No delivery hassles. No waiting. No inventory shortages. Want it? It's yours.

Although you might not opt for the general nature of a flea market, you might be smart to market at a specialized fair. With either, many guerrillas have discovered that they can earn maxi profits in mini time.

SPECIAL EVENTS

There are three reasons guerrillas profit by marketing through special events:

1. Their best customers and prospects tend to attend these gatherings.
2. They frequently generate free media coverage if the event is special enough.
3. They strengthen their relationships with their prime customers, setting the stage for customer loyalty.

Special events take a multitude of formats, from special sales to unveilings. Imaginative guerrillas create special events, at which the above three guerrilla glories are bestowed upon them, by staging such goings-on as:

- Clinics on features and benefits of new offerings
- Seminars and workshops right on the premises
- Presentations by famous people or experts
- Parties celebrating anything but anniversaries
- Fund-raising parties to benefit local charities
- Contests for kids, attracting local TV stations
- Contests for grown-ups, attracting local TV stations
- Plaques and trophies awarded to appropriate people
- Launching community activities, reeking of altruism

All of these special events have the possibility of attracting customers, coverage, and cash flow. Perhaps you'll go all out to ensure the success of these events by advertising them in the newspaper or in the electronic media. Possibly you'll have searchlights illuminating the skies on the night of your special event.

You can add to the festiveness with free commemorative gifts, refreshments (but not of the boozy variety unless your judgment tells you otherwise), clowns, mimes, video cameras recording the event for later showing, live music, entertaining demonstrations of your offering, and local celebrities. You want profits. Mayors want votes.

Special events are part of a brilliant marketing plan. They are preplanned months, often years, in advance. As I write this, I am signed and sealed, booked to be part of a company's special event two years and three months from today.

You might want to plan events as frequently as quarterly or as infrequently as every two years. Twice a year is a good target—if you have the logistics, person power, and the reasons to stage special events.

Be sure you concentrate on getting media coverage—especially from the local newspapers, because although the event will last a few hours, reprints of the publicity can last forever in your other marketing materials.

Searchlights and Blimps

When the idea is not to sell your benefits, but to call attention to yourself, few marketing vehicles do the trick with the pizzazz of searchlights and blimps. That's probably why you're seeing more and more of them these days. (Remember when the only blimps used to be for a tire company? Now you see them for soft drinks, film, and who knows what else.)

Billboards on trucks, sort of highway versions of blimps, are coming down the pike, but searchlights, which carry no message, and blimps, which carry both names and messages, are far more commonplace.

Let's deal with these skybound allies of guerrillas separately, because they certainly offer different kinds of benefits.

Searchlights call attention to the fact that an event is going on *right now*. Searchlights are limited to nighttime use. And their prime purpose is to generate attention. Speaking of generate—a searchlight is ordinarily a large light on wheels connected to a large generator on wheels. The cost varies, but it's in the neighborhood of $100 to $300 per hour, with a four-hour minimum. Searchlights are associated with sales, and those who have used them report they pay for themselves in most cases. If not, I doubt if you can blame the searchlight.

After all, it's only going to flag the attention of people driving by or living in the neighborhood. A surprise about searchlights: If you plan to use one, know that the generator that powers it is loud.

Blimps, which are far more costly, are also quite loud. In the past, we had one famous blimp. These days we have many. And some of them rent their blimpside space to advertisers and then cruise overhead, attracting attention and implanting a name.

At night, some of these blimps feature bright, moving words that flash your message to countless earthbound prospects.

I doubt if any marketing campaign can be built solely on searchlights and blimps, but the key to guerrilla marketing is a rich marketing mix. And I know that searchlights and blimps can be welcome ingredients in the mix. So can helium-filled inflatables, which can be made in almost any form. Like a shoe? Yes. A book? Yes. How 'bout a car? Yes again. Inflatables are attention-getting and economical.

You might even consider owning your own blimp if it seems especially well targeted to your audience, if you can find a place to keep it, if you can locate someone to fly it, and if you can find a way to rent the blimpside space to guerrillas like you who wish to beam their messages from places that are devoid of most media.

SEMINARS AND WORKSHOPS

A fast-growing, highly flexible, and promising new method of marketing is the giving of seminars or workshops. Now, I'm not talking about the kind of seminars where you earn a profit on the seminar and the sale of literature, tapes, and services at the end of the seminar.

Nothing against that kind. But I'm talking, guerrilla to guerrilla, about seminars as marketing tools. I mean free seminars—though you might charge a small fee to cover your costs—at which you give valuable, free information—including a bit about why the people attending should buy what you sell.

Make this marketing weapon work for you by running ads in newspapers, announcing the seminar. The ideal advertising for your seminar would begin two weeks before you deliver it. Run a second ad one week before; run two more ads on the two days before you hold it.

When holding the seminar or workshop, offer it at two different times of day. Twelve noon and seven in the evening have been successful. Scheduling like this works weekdays. Saturdays are also good days for free seminars.

At your seminar, which should be planned for one hour, devote the first forty-five minutes to giving helpful, solid, valuable information. Devote the next fifteen minutes to selling the benefits of your product or service. You'll do best if you realize that you will be delivering a fifteen-minute live commercial.

If you did a great job the first forty-five minutes and an equally superlative job the final fifteen minutes, you can expect up to 33 percent of the people to end up buying what you are selling.

Successful companies raise that percentage in one of three ways, and sometimes all three ways:

1. They have a different person take the stage the final fifteen minutes—a real pro at motivating crowds.
2. They have salespeople at the doorways, selling to the people as they leave (the room is arranged so that the people must pass a salesperson).
3. They make a very special offer available on that day only.

MERCHANDISE DISPLAYS

Because so many purchase decisions are made in the unconscious part of the mind, merchandise displays are powerful tools in triggering impulse reactions. The Point-of-Purchase Institute reports that seven of ten purchase decisions are made right at the point of sale, emphasizing even more the crucial importance of merchandise displays. Each display should contain both product and copy.

These displays should clearly present the product or products for sale, along with a message about them directed to customers within the store. This message, which ordinarily appears above the display—in the case of a display bin, on a special sign called a "header card"—should tie in with your (or the product's) current marketing theme as it appears outside the store. In addition, it should tell the customer exactly what to do. Examples: "Buy three; get one free" or "Get your Acme Widget today!"

Merchandise displays must always look neat, but should never be full. If they are, customers will assume that nobody else is buying the products and that making the purchase might be a mistake. Instead, have several products missing to communicate nonverbally that others have been buying. When not using a display bin, try to arrange your merchandise display so your products appear at eye level.

When using a bin, do what you can to have it located near the cash register, where the maximum number of impulse reactions can be generated. Location is even more important than an organized display. But neither factor should be neglected.

The display should be colorful, clean, and brightly illuminated. It should be straightened out frequently to look neat. The typeface used in the message should be clearly readable from a distance of ten feet or more. Don't forget that merchandise displays should be designed not only to focus the attention of people near the display but also to attract the attention of those far from the display.

Moving displays work better than stationary displays because of their ability to attract attention. Rotating displays enable you to present the maximum number of products. And if you can arrange for a video monitor to play a continuous loop videotape at the display, you are acting like a true guerrilla, availing yourself of state-of-the-moment display tools.

If you cannot use a display bin of your own, try to have signs of any kind around your display; the more you tell, the more you sell. A merchandise display should be a silent salesperson for your product. If possible, show the product in use and the benefits of using the product. Many guerrilla manufacturers provide displays to retailers for free with orders of a minimum size, so if you're a retailer, ask for them. And if you're a manufacturer, offer them. They work.

DEMONSTRATIONS

Few guerrilla marketing weapons are as powerful and convincing as demonstrations. Demos allow your prospect to see what it would be like to own your product or employ your service. Demos break through the marketing BS detectors with which so many Americans are now equipped.

You can conduct your demonstrations at trade shows, consumer shows, fairs, exhibits, and conferences. You can perform them in the office or home of your prospect—or in your own place of business.

Demonstrations are constantly being conducted in stores, in store windows—even on television. In fact, one of TV's greatest assets is its ability to demonstrate your product or service in action.

Naturally, the thing to demonstrate is your product or service. But the thing to emphasize is the *benefit* to your prospect. Let the features and benefits of your offering speak for themselves. They are far more eloquent than the words of even the highest-paid copywriters.

But they still can be abetted by your helpful words, pointing out the features, pointing out the benefits, directing the prospects' attention to the speed or convenience or economy or hidden values of your offering.

It makes sense that the best time to close a sale is immediately after the demonstration. There is little else you can do to prove the merits of your product—other than showing testimonial letters, offering a special price, and proving that your offering has received community or industry acceptance.

Demonstrations can often extinguish the most harsh sales objections—if the demos are convincing and impressive. For proof, just talk to any auto dealer, most of whom do all in their power to give their prospects a test drive—the ultimate demonstration of a car.

Demonstrations should be accompanied by a sales presentation, but it is usually an error to leave behind a brochure after giving the demonstration. If you didn't make the sale with the demo, the brochure is a less potent weapon. Also, the brochure is a nifty excuse for the prospect to postpone the sale by saying "Let me look over your brochure before I decide."

Some may decide to buy after perusing the brochure. But far more will not. Most people will buy from guerrillas who realize that the time to close is right after the demonstration. If folks are not impressed then, you're in deep trouble.

CONSULTATIONS

Along with sampling, demonstrations, and free seminars, free consultations are one of the most cost-effective weapons in a guerrilla's arsenal.

They prove your expertise; they help you establish a relationship; they give your prospect the closest idea of what it would be like to buy what you are selling. Best of all, they do this at a minimum risk to you with very little out-of-pocket expense, if any.

One of the most winning aspects of free consultations is your ability to offer them—in your brochures, mailings, or ads—for *free*, a word with enormous emotional impact.

During your consultation, which should occur at your place of business if seeing it would positively influence the prospect, or at the client's office if convenience is paramount, you should earnestly set your sights on satisfying the prospect and providing him or her with the maximum amount of service, information, help, and understanding.

You do not do consultations to sell yourself. You do them to prove yourself, and in doing so you happen to sell yourself. The focal point is your prospect, not you.

Keep your free consultations down to a one-hour maximum. More than that is unnecessary and actually demeans the worth of your time. Less than that is shortchanging everyone.

Naturally, you don't want to give your prospect a million dollars' worth of information and aid, unless you have $100 million more in reserve. But you do want to impress the prospect with your intelligence, customer orientation, effectiveness, efficiency, timeliness, authority, experience, and ability to build the prospect's profits or improve the prospect's life.

After the one-hour free consultation, you should ask for the order or get the prospect to sign on your dotted line. Or, you can leave quietly and attempt to close the sale by mail and phone shortly afterward—very shortly.

Consider yourself fortunate if you have a business that lends itself to the offering of free consultations. It helps establish the momentum that leads to the sale, and it does so in a manner that entices prospects because of its honesty and freedom from making a mistake. If you said your consultation would be one hour, after that, offer to leave. If you are invited to stay, that's fine. And if your client offers to pay, that's fine, too. But keep your promise of a free one-hour consultation to establish your integrity.

Even if you start by closing only 25 percent of consultations, polish your consultations so that you can close 100 percent.

SALES PRESENTATIONS

A sales presentation takes anywhere from twenty seconds to two hours—and sometimes longer. The best of all sales presentations are memorized. Guerrilla marketers know that 20 percent of their salespeople make 80 percent of their sales.

So they actually audiotape and videotape those superstars and play the tapes for the 80 percent who aren't pulling their weight. The 80 percent learn from the materials that top salespeople use certain words and phrases, and specific voice inflections.

The 80 percent also see that the top 20 percent use special nonverbal communications that transform prospects into customers. They use these words, phrases, inflections, and physical mannerisms to increase their own sales productivity.

If they have memorized the sales presentation so well that it appears to come directly from the heart and not seem memorized, they—and the sales manager—have done their job properly. Sales rise accordingly.

The best sales presentations come right after an initial contact, where a human bond is formed. They also have visual aids—because points made to the eye and ear are more effective than points made to the ear alone. The best presentations are oriented to the customer, are centered on the benefits of the product or service being sold, and are loaded with information.

As top salespeople through the years have learned, the more you tell, the more you sell. A great sales presentation is also peppered with attempts to close the sale. The close need not come at the end of the presentation, but can come in the middle of the presentation as well.

After a presentation is made, a gold-medal salesperson does a bang-up job of listening, then attempts to close based upon the remarks made by the prospect.

Sales presentations are often the heart and soul of great marketing. Great marketing can usually get a prospect to a place where he or she wants to hear the presentation, but it's the presentation itself that closes the loop and completes the sale.

Do prospects enjoy hearing sales presentations? They love it! They enjoy being singled out and told the features and benefits of the offering. They appreciate the attention.

Be sure you take full advantage of this magic moment in marketing. Make your sales presentation complete, centered on the prospect, and aided by visuals and demonstrations. Enthusiasm and sincerity fuel great sales presentations—and if you've got quality in your product or service, both enthusiasm and sincerity should be easy to come by.

Direct-Mail Letters

The fastest-growing segment in marketing during the 1980s was direct marketing. That included letters, postcards, brochures, newspaper or magazine coupons, telemarketing, canvassing, and TV or radio direct-response commercials.

A guerrilla selects a combination from this high-powered selection, then makes his or her offer repeatedly. One of the most potent weapons in the direct-marketing arsenal is direct-mail letters. Here are ten hints for using them well:

1. Save money by incurring no high production costs.
2. Give enough data, in letters from one to twelve pages long, for prospects to make an informed decision to buy.
3. Do as much personalizing as possible. Personalize name, town, special interests, and anything else you can.
4. State your offer right in the beginning, again in the middle, and once more at the end.
5. Always create a sense of urgency by giving prospects a cutoff date by which time they must respond to your offer.
6. Always include a P.S. The P.S. is the second thing readers read, following only the opening line.
7. Stress your main points with underlines, bold type, all caps, or a yellow highlighter effect. But don't stress too much.
8. Use short paragraphs, sentences, and words. In letters of two or more pages, use subheads.
9. Use black ink plus blue to underline, print your signature, and even make margin notes or "handwrite" a P.S.
10. Tell the reader exactly what to do upon completing the letter, along with how to do it and when to do it.

A guerrilla direct-marketing campaign might consist of four pieces sent at two-week intervals: a two-page letter, then a one-page letter, then a postcard, then a telephone follow-up.

All guerrillas know that even the best letters don't get read if the envelope doesn't get opened. So knock yourself out to get recipients to open it. This may be accomplished with a typed address (no label) plus a stamp; with a "teaser" line printed on the outside, motivating the person to open it; with a window that shows a reason to open the envelope (photo of free gift, resemblance to a check, or a unique design).

Hard-core guerrillas affix eight stamps to their letters: one six-center, two four-centers, one three-center, and four two-centers. The total is still twenty-five cents. But you know it's impossible to ignore a letter with eight stamps stuck on it. Once again, time, energy, and imagination triumph over pure megabucks. Can you imagine a Fortune 500 company taking the time to send eight-stamp letters?

Many guerrillas have an arsenal of letters for different occasions: promotions, offers, thank-yous, follow-ups, referral-seekers, and more. Test direct-mail letters till you have a fileful of proven winners.

Direct-Mail Postcards

One of the most effective, inexpensive, proven, and reliable methods of marketing is direct-mail postcards. Direct mail itself has three goals:

1. To be opened
2. To be read
3. To get the order

Direct-mail postcards achieve the first two goals automatically.

Amazingly inexpensive to use, especially when you use them with your own customer list, postcards enable you to make your offer and be confident it will generate profits (if it's a good offer).

Your postcard should stand out in some way—either with an outstanding design or by the use of huge, compelling headline words. Be sure it tells recipients exactly what they are to do: visit a location, make a phone call, look for a display, mail something back, some concrete action.

Be brief, but if your offer is enticing, readers will want enough information to buy, so don't be skimpy with the facts. Use your postcard to show something if you can.

Want a key thought to remember? Here's one: Don't think in terms of a postcard mailing; think in terms of a series of postcard mailings. Still, one-shot mailings work for sales.

If you're going to mail to many people, open your mind to full-color postcards. A giant oversize full-color postcard measuring five by eight inches with full color on one side and 150 words of copy on the other runs only $679 in quantities of five thousand. That's a mite over 13 cents each. A standard three-by-five-inch postcard with full color runs $365 for five thousand—7.3 cents each.

You can also get fancy and have a built-in response device with your postcard, a smart idea. Double-panel postcards cost $740 for five thousand. The costs are not as prohibitive as you may have thought. Delivery takes about four weeks. These prices are from but one supplier, Norman Printing, which invites you to call collect at 916-877-2335.

If you're going to go the postcard route, try to use the front to "tease" readers into reading the back. On the back, put your main offer into a headline. Try to put forth a time-limited offer so that people must respond by a certain date to take you up on your special offer—and so that you can measure the response rate of your mailing.

Because of the low cost, simplicity, elimination of an envelope, and opportunity to make an offer instantly, I am very high on postcards.

I've seen clients cut mailing costs in half while doubling response rates. If you have a customer list, you can do the same. Cutting your marketing costs while raising your profits is a goal of this book. Direct-mail postcards will help both of us attain that goal.

Postcard Decks

The fastest-growing segment of fast-growing direct marketing is postcard decks, groups of postcards mailed in plastic envelopes, each offering products and services.

These postcard decks can be targeted at virtually any consumer group: homeowners, housewives, parents, psychologists, affluent people, business owners, and a whole lot more. Weekly, new groups are added.

Offers on these postcards—or coupons, as they are also accurately described—range from discounts on merchandise to free consultations to full-color brochures to free meals.

Small businesses are attracted to postcard decks because of high response rates, from 5 to 15 percent, and low cost—usually around a nickel each, including design, layout, typesetting, printing, and mailing.

You can get more information on postcard decks by calling R.S.V.P. at (415) 485-0996. You'll learn that some deck publishers offer full-color printing and others don't. Some support each mailing with radio and TV announcements.

If you're going to capitalize on this low-cost form of direct marketing, consider what your offer might be. The offer is key. Examples: A recent postcard deck mailing to me contained offers from around the whole nation for free catalogs, a free dental consultation, a reduced-rate hotel suite, a free design appointment, a 10 percent discount, a multitude of free brochures, a bargain weekend in San Francisco, a specially priced dinner for two, a 40 percent discount, a chance to get on a mailing list, and a free shirt if I bought five. There were a whopping thirty-one postcards in the deck.

Large and small businesses were advertised. Local and national. Products and services. New and old firms. Some had been included in past postcard deck mailings. Others were newcomers. As you can tell, word is spreading.

Most decks contain actual postcards, which recipients return to request the free enticement. These are usually not postage-paid. Other decks contain only coupons, not postcards. Their offers are similar to those made on postcards, but people have to present them in person in order to get the special deal.

This kind of group marketing has been going on since the 1970s, so even though you may not yet have experimented with it, you most likely have received a few postcard decks. Because 89 percent of companies who try them continue to market with postcards in decks, you've got to assume they work. Everyone I know who has employed this weapon says so. How about you?

Booths for Malls

You don't have to invest heavily to have a second location. Or even a fifty-second location. A portable booth, constructed of wood or plastic, can do the job nicely.

You can put it in a mall, in a hypermarket, in a parking lot, at a fair, in a show, or even in a large showroom.

These days, if you've ever visited a *hypermarket*—a huge collection of stores under one roof—you'll see portable booths at which a wide variety of products and services are sold. I'm talking about the full gamut from dentistry to poultry, from fine art to legal advice.

In most cases, you've got to contribute a fair share of your gross to the owner of the premises. But the cost should feel just and proper to you because of the enormous number of people who will pass your place of business—and buy your offerings, if you've got good signage, good prices, and good quality.

Some businesses feel they must first have a "flagship" store in a standard location such as a mall or downtown street. But many guerrillas have no such rent to pay. Portable booths are their only location—or locations.

If you can't construct the booth with your own two hands, call one of the display designers conveniently listed in your yellow pages. Those people have the expertise in marketing that you don't often find with general contractors.

They'll be able to construct a booth that provides you with the maximum inventory space, marketing space, display area, and employee comfort. Unlike many edifices, your portable booth will probably display signs both inside and out, on all possible walls. It will display most merchandise from the walls as well.

One of the major joys of a portable booth is that if one location doesn't work out, you simply move to a location that does. Later, you can add a second location, a third, a fourth. . . .

Each booth must be staffed by a person with a quick mind, able to think spontaneously because of the large amount of people with whom he or she will come in contact. Your representative must be able to answer questions without phoning headquarters. You may not even have a headquarters—or a telephone. The booth must be capable of being locked securely because booths are much easier to burgle than standard locations.

But if this strategy works out for you, you'll glorify the day you made the one-time investment in your first portable booth.

Doorhangers

Doorhangers don't hang doors. Instead, they hang on door-knobs. This means they're marketing messages hung on the front door of a residence. The law prohibits you from stuffing your materials into mailboxes, but most communities do not legally frown on doorhangers.

These low-priced marketing weapons can do a variety of jobs for you: entice people into your store, tempt them into ordering your product, motivate them to call you for more information, remind them of your other marketing efforts, and give enough data for them to come learn more about what you are selling.

Some doorhangers are simple, two-sided, rectangular minibrochures capable of hanging from a doorknob. Others are more ornate and may be a packet of marketing materials, all in a plastic bag that hangs from a front door. Although you may want to do the hanging job yourself, many firms employ high school students to do the hanging for them.

The primary advantage of doorhangers are that they are inexpensive, that they reach people at their homes (ideal if your offering is also for the home), that they enable you to geographically zero in on prospects, and that they have little competition—unlike direct mail, which must compete for the prospect's attention with a multitude of other mail.

Probably the best use of doorhangers that I've seen was by a guerrilla who hired high school students to blanket a neighborhood with doorhangers—each of which contained a brief sales pitch, then a phone number to call for more information. The 18 percent (!) who responded were soon visited by a college student who closed the sale.

The doorhanger couldn't do the whole marketing task. But it did open the door (pun intended) to a person who could.

These particular doorhangers, unlike the usual black-and-white el cheapo variety, were glossy and produced in full color. The guerrilla using them wanted his identity to be conveyed in all of his marketing materials. The doorhangers did a dandy job of establishing that identity right at the get-go. Not very inexpensive, but very effective. Ask any direct mailer how he'd feel at an 18 percent response. Save your time; I can tell you: he'd feel marvelous.

Glean from this example the idea that doorhangers can start the momentum that leads to the closed sale. As part of a campaign, they can be a valuable cog. Doorhangers are not overused. So they are not resented by the folks who live behind the doors. If the offer is exciting enough, doorhangers are appreciated. If yours is a home-oriented product or service, consider testing the efficacy of doorhangers. They have worked for many a guerrilla.

SALES REPRESENTATIVES

In many companies, the best sales representatives earn more than the president of the company, and the president is delighted at their success. The president knows that these sales reps are the place where sales are won and lost. Marketing can only attract prospects; it usually takes a top sales representative to transform prospect into customer.

First-rate sales representatives have five things in common:

1. They love to sell.
2. They enjoy people.
3. They have a sincere and high degree of enthusiasm.
4. They know their product and their prospects.
5. They believe they will close every sale.

These winning sales representatives are dressed in a manner to inspire confidence. They are so neat and clean that the prospect unconsciously assumes the entire company has its act equally together and buttoned up. They talk clearly, rapidly, use gestures, smile, and engage in eye contact. In addition, they use the prospect's name whenever possible. And they orient all their remarks to that prospect.

Although great sales reps are born that way, they can also be trained to be great. Repeated sales training—by way of videotape, audiotape, newsletter, memo, and in-person—is how this happens. Great sales reps would rather be out in the field selling than sitting in an office or even running the company. They love the action and gratification that comes with closing a sale—and helping their prospect.

Your sales force will probably be judged by its weakest rep. Perhaps that rep works for you. Or maybe he or she works for a sales rep organization that represents you. Still, the personification of your company appears in the form of that representative. So you've got to be sure the rep would make you proud in appearance, attire, words, and attitude.

Throughout America, 20 percent of all salespeople make 80 percent of all sales. It is your job to raise the expertise of your lower 80 percent to that of the top 20 percent. Consistent sales training is the way to do it.

The best of all sales representatives have studied the product or service they are selling, the competition, and the target prospects so well that they glow when they are selling. Their enthusiasm and confidence are contagious.

They are clearly proud of their offering, their company, and themselves. They do not consider selling to be work. Instead, they look on it as a service to their customers, and they enjoy doing it. They literally feel they are doing their customers a favor by making the sale. To sales reps like that, selling is a breeze, never a chore. May your staff be blessed with many of them.

9

WEAPONS THAT HAVE EXTRA FIREPOWER

The mass media, well known by advertisers to have extra firepower because they reach so many targets, were long out of the domain of the entrepreneur. The costs were clearly prohibitive.

Owners of new and small businesses, who needed advertising to help establish their reputations, were denied this turnpike to credibility because the tolls were too high. It was very difficult to afford a single ad or commercial, much less an entire advertising campaign.

Although those notions are now part of history and have little pertinence in the present, many business owners continue to be intimidated at the very thought of magazines. Say the phrase "full-page magazine ad" to them and they blanch. Mention running commercials on prime-time television and their eyes glaze over. This is definitely something that they'd like to do, but they have the old-fashioned idea that there is no way they can afford it.

Now, however, advertising has changed, become more accessible to the small business owner. Newspapers offer zone editions, magazines offer regional editions, radio offers package prices, television offers cable opportunities, and even billboards offer single board leases.

A new word describes the mass media. Entrepreneurs love this word. It is *affordable*.

Of the 7 weapons assessed in this chapter, advertising is the first because it is the most general—and if misused, the most expensive. But you wouldn't consider advertising expensive if you invested $1,000 in an ad and received $10,000 in profits as a result.

Ask a nonguerrilla what marketing is and that person will most likely answer that it is advertising. Luckily I'm on hand to alert you to the plain fact that advertising is one one-hundredth of marketing, an important part, to be sure, but not the end-all and be-all. Still, there is little question that it belongs in any chapter dealing with extra firepower. Advertising reaches thousands, and maybe millions, while smiles and sales presentations reach but one at a time.

Accomplished with intelligence and flair, and strategically combined with other weapons of guerrilla marketing, advertising can develop another weapon for you.

That weapon, also possessed of awesome firepower, is your reputation. Reputations can be created faster than you might imagine. Good ones take longer to create than bad ones, which grow in a hurry. I guess it's an American pastime to pass along bad word-of-mouth.

A good reputation means credibility, positive word-of-mouth, confidence, and profits. It means you've become a brand name, a trusted business. Reputations don't just happen. You create them.

There's a wonderful old adage akin to this: "Life eats people. Or people eat life."

In terms of your business reputation, do the things necessary, all described in this book, to earn the kind of reputation you want. Eat life. Don't be a side dish.

After looking into advertising and reputation as high-potency weapons of the savvy guerrilla, Chapter 9 explores

the most common of all the weapons with extra firepower—
newspaper advertising. It's too important to do poorly.

Magazine ads are packed with plenty of firepower, too.
And they're available in national, regional, local, city, business, and trade editions—so you can aim at national, regional, local, city, business, or trade targets. To gain the
most insight into magazines, spend half a day at a good
library curled up with the current consumer magazine edition of *Standard Rate and Data Service.* Ask the reference
librarian to point it out, then get set for many happy
surprises. But you can begin your journey to magazine wisdom just a few pages ahead in *Guerrilla Marketing Weapons.*

Radio commercials are a topic on which you may already
consider yourself an expert, having heard so many, probably too many. But as a guerrilla, it will be worth your time
to read a bit about radio spots, to see if they may be for
you, and if so, to learn how to make them work hardest—
meaning: to sell the most.

Television commercials are the most powerful of the
ultrapowerful weapons. They come at you from all fronts—
sound, sight, logic, emotion, demonstration. High firepower
and, once upon a time, high prices, too, were part of
television. But in 1990, thanks to the nearly 70 percent of
American homes hooked up to cable TV, high prices are
no longer part of the equation. As recently as 1980, 90
percent of those homes were tuned to networks during
prime time. In 1990, the figure dropped to almost 65 percent.

Does it seem to you that marketing is moving in a direction that favors small businesses, especially those run by
guerrillas? It seems that way to me.

Outdoor billboards, specifically those at busy intersec-
tions or on well-traveled highways, have loads of firepower.
If your audience is in their cars, zipping past the billboards
—as I was the other day when I drove past a billboard
advertising a radio station, then immediately turned to that
station—gain the benefits these blights on the horizon—not
all horizons, but some—can provide for your company.

Now that you're wrapping your mind around marketing, open it to the possibility of using weapons with extra firepower. There are few substitutes for multiple bull's-eyes and few methods for scoring them other than those upcoming. Use them with accuracy and professionalism, or don't use them at all.

Advertising

As important as advertising is, it is only one percent of the entire marketing process and it is entirely possible, though not often, to market without any advertising at all. You might sell your entire output at one trade show.

Most of the time, however, advertising is necessary. This is true for five main reasons:

1. It establishes credibility for your business.
2. It gives you a forum to show and state your advantages.
3. It allows you to repeat your message and gain access to the unconscious minds of your prospects and customers.
4. It allows you to communicate with many people at a relatively inexpensive cost, compared with sales calls.
5. It lets you target your prospects, and test your product.

The most important point to remember about advertising is that it is really a fancy way for saying *selling*. Many people think it is the entire marketing process, when it is only part of the process. Many others expect miracles and instant results from it. Alas, advertising provides neither.

Unless you engage in direct-response advertising, such as making a special time-limited offer like a sale, it takes a bit of time for advertising's effect to be felt.

Figure that if you advertise regularly, about three to four months will pass before you feel those first effects. They should improve every month thereafter—provided you continue advertising regularly. After about twelve months of advertising, you can stop entirely for two months without any accompanying dropoff in sales. But don't go longer than two months. Remember that stopping your advertising to save money is a bit like stopping your watch to save time.

Whether you engage in print, electronic, or direct-mail advertising, the basic rules remain the same:

1. Your ad should be built around an idea.
2. The headline or opening line is the most important.
3. Tell people exactly what you want them to do.
4. Focus your advertising on benefits to customers.
5. The key to advertising success is commitment.

Once you've selected a medium or a few media for your advertising, stay with them and don't switch around. A lot of small ads or short commercials are better than one big ad or long commercial. But be certain that you give your prospects enough information to make a purchase decision.

Advertising works best when it is teamed with other marketing weapons such as direct mail, signs, public relations, and involvement with your community or industry. Of all marketing expenses, the highest amount in the United States goes to advertising.

REPUTATION

Reputations are a whole lot easier to destroy than to build. It takes years to build a reputation, but mere days to kill it. One way to destroy it is by not realizing the customer is always right—even when the customer is dead wrong.

Another way is with poor service. Slow order processing is another way. Shoddy-looking marketing materials can damage a reputation, as can the presence of exaggeration or, worse yet, dishonesty in your marketing. And you well know that poor quality can hurt your reputation. Still another way that enters my mind is communicating an image that is a long way from your honest identity.

Poor word-of-mouth spreads faster than wildfire. If one person has a bad experience with your company, an average of twenty-two others will hear about it. Thirteen percent of the people spread the bad word to forty more folks. You may have spent ten years building that reputation, but it can become irreparably damaged by one unpleasant incident with one person. Be careful! Your reputation is one of your most precious assets.

You build a successful reputation in a variety of ways. Let's examine five:

1. You advertise in a regional edition of a respected national magazine, then make reprints, which you use for years. The result is instant credibility, which equates with reputation.
2. You are a consistent advertiser, using the same media and running ads that inspire confidence in prospects.
3. You bend over backward to offer the ultimate in convenience: hours open, days of operation, efficient phone service, availability of financing, all credit cards accepted, a deep respect for your customers' time.
4. You write a column for a local or industry publica-

tion, give seminars on your topic of expertise, publish a valuable newsletter for customers and prospects.

5. You make sure that every one of your employees reveres customer relations as much as you do. If customer love ends with you, your reputation is in danger. Everyone must feel it. Everyone must show it. Even on Mondays and Fridays.

By constantly putting those principles into practice, you cannot help but develop a healthy reputation. Companies with good reputations rarely surprise their customers. They are known quantities and that is the foundation of their reputations. People know, trust, and patronize them.

Begin immediately to do what you can to earn the kind of reputation that leads to repeat business and high profits.

Newspaper Ads

Whether you are interested in national, local, or community newspapers, think in terms of using them consistently. And that means no less than once a week.

Generally, the best day to run a newspaper ad is a Sunday, when people take the most time to read the paper. Monday is a good day if your audience is primarily male—because all the weekend sports are summarized in the Monday paper. Friday is a good day if your business picks up on weekends. Wednesday and Thursday are good days if those are the food days in your paper and yours is a food-related offering. And Saturday is an excellent day since few advertisers use the Saturday edition, thinking it is a day of poor readership. That means less competition for your prospects' attention and money.

To gain the maximum overall readership, request that your ad run in the main news section, as far forward as possible, on a right-hand page near the right margin and above the fold. To dominate a page, which is usually eight columns wide and twenty-two inches high, design an ad that is five columns wide and twelve or more inches high. You should also look into the use of adding one color, since almost any color helps your ad to stand out. And whatever you do, don't let the newspaper design your ad, because it will end up looking like many other newspaper ads.

People read the newspaper to learn the news, so make your ad as newsy as possible. If your ad is small, give it a distinctive border so it creates a visual identity for your ads. Be sure to give your prospects enough data to buy what you are selling. Don't fall into the trap of revering "white space" because it looks good. Your ads are supposed to win sales, not design awards.

Once you've selected a newspaper that is read by your

prospects, stick with that newspaper. But don't expect it to work instantly unless you make a limited-time offer—such as a free gift for coming in to your place of business by a certain date, or a time-dated coupon offering a special discount price. And see if your newspaper offers regional editions, targeted for your geographic area. More and more papers are offering this service to economy-minded advertisers.

Be sure your graphics designer produces the ad in a way in which it will reproduce well in the newspaper or newspapers you have selected. Often that means using straightforward type and no "reversing" of white type against a black background.

The first thing people see in your ad will be the headline, which should tell the story or entice the reader into learning more. Next, people see the main visual, the subhead, and then your name. So make your name and theme line prominent. Try to put your main offer into your headline or subhead so that even those who do not read the copy will get the main point. The lifeblood of many small businesses is newspaper advertising, so commit to it long enough for it to work its selling wonders for you.

Magazine Ads

People become involved with magazines more than with other media. This means they'll also be likely to become involved with your magazine ad. The lesson there is to put forth a lot of data.

People also associate the credibility of the magazine with the advertiser. So a new company advertising in an established magazine can frequently shorten the time it takes to gain consumer confidence.

If you advertise in business magazines, you'll be less likely to find the money-saving regional editions you find in national magazines. For example, a full-page ad in *Time* may cost $50,000 in the national edition, but only $1,500 in a local edition. What's more, people reading the local edition do not know it is local, so they are quite impressed with the company you'll be keeping in that magazine.

Small advertisers can gain big mileage from magazines by requesting reprints of their ad that read something like "As seen in *Time* magazine." They then can use those reprints as mailers, as part of mailings, as signs, as posters (as blowups), and as easel-back window and counter displays. Even if they only run the ad one time, they can continue using the reprints for years afterward.

Some magazines offer both display and classified sections to advertisers, and they offer special discounts to mail-order advertisers. To gain deep insight into magazines, check your library for a copy of *Standard Rate and Data Service's Directory of Consumer Magazines*. This valuable volume tells you rates, regional editions, demographics, circulation figures, and discount structures. It also lists many magazines that might be appropriate and affordable, yet unknown to you.

Before deciding whether to use color or black and white, bleed (an ad that goes to the edge of the page without a margin) or nonbleed, a quarter-page ad, a full-page ad, or a two-page spread, be sure your ad is first centered on a powerful and clear idea. Then let that idea dictate the use of color and size.

Remember that one of the main reasons for using magazines is their ability to target in on your audience. As with other media, consistency of exposure is important—unless you intentionally run your ad one time only in order to gain the benefit of the many low-cost merchandising aids made available by the magazine. If you run a coupon ad, be sure your address appears not only on the coupon but elsewhere, too—just in case someone clips the coupon and someone else wants to respond to your offer. But these days, with toll-free numbers, coupons seem to be disappearing. Use the space some other way.

Another of the prime advantages of magazines is their large "pass-along" readership. Unlike newspapers, which get tossed out the next day, magazines tend to stay around longer. But to a guerrilla, the name of the magazine game is big-time credibility.

Radio Commercials

Radio is the most intimate of the mass media, generally occurring as a one-on-one situation. Keeping this thought in mind will help you write or judge more effective commercials.

As is any kind of marketing, a radio commercial is based on an idea—not a song, singer, theme line, or sound effect. The idea should be stated at the beginning of the commercial, during the middle, and at the end. State it in any words you wish—varying them, if you'd like, each time you state them. Just be sure you're stating the same idea.

Because radio is a relatively low-impact medium, you need to make many impressions to influence a purchase decision. As a bare minimum, think of running five commercials per day, four days a week, three weeks out of every four. As a better gauge, think of ten commericals per day, four days a week, three weeks out of every four. The commercials should have the feel of a whole campaign—with a cohesive identity. This may be carried forward by the announcer, music, format, theme, or offer.

As a general rule, advertisers should view radio in two basic categories: foreground stations, as exemplified by talk shows, news shows, religious shows, or sports shows; and background stations, the kind that play music.

Listeners *actively* listen to foreground stations while they *passively* listen to background stations. Result? Your commercial has a greater chance of being ignored by people who are tuned in for the music, not the chatter.

If you're going to use "personality" radio, try to get the personality to try your product or service, then add his or her real-life comments. The testimonial value of this radio tactic is inestimable. Perhaps you can get a local (or national) celebrity to deliver the words in your commercial in a trade for whatever you make, sell, or perform. Just be sure the celebrity doesn't get in the way of the sales talk.

Happily, the cost of a radio campaign is less than you think. The best radio commercials attempt to put across one basic idea, not more than that. They repeat and repeat and repeat again the name of the product or service because they are created with the cognizance that most of the audience isn't paying that much attention. The worst radio commercials usually have the best music—music so excellent that nobody pays any attention to the words, just to the music.

Music increases the depth of penetration of your radio message. And if you have millions to hammer home your jingle, the rules are different. For guerrillas, radio commercials serve as a strong support medium in a marketing mix. Although radio has been known to do the entire selling job, generally it cannot function as the sole form of marketing. So rely on it to help, but recognize that it is known as a low-impact marketing weapon.

TV Commercials

We are now dealing with the undisputed heavyweight champion of marketing. TV commercials enable you to:

- Reach thousands, millions, or tens of millions of people at the same time.
- Demonstrate your product or service before the eyes of the viewers.
- Use drama, music, close-ups, special effects, comparisons, and more to convey your benefits and identity.
- Reach the right-brained people, who are influenced by emotional, aesthetic appeals; and the left-brained folks, who respond to logical, sequential reasoning.
- Put your product or service on the tube for as little as fifteen seconds or as long as two minutes—even longer.

In preguerrilla days, TV intimidated the small business owner. But now, with the advent of cable TV and satellite TV, the cost of commercials has plummeted to lower than $10 on some stations, lower than $5 on many more. The cost of producing a commercial—making a thirty-second movie—averaged $156,000 in 1989. But it can cost as little as $1,000 with proper planning.

When you think of TV, think of your target audience. Run your spots on the shows they watch, at the times they watch. Using TV correctly means running several spots a day, several days a week, several weeks a month—and sometimes every month of the year, though that is not always necessary.

TV is a visual medium with audio enhancement. It is not a radio commercial with pictures. Judge your commercial by seeing if you understand the main point even if the sound is off. Be sure your name is clearly communicated. These days, people use their remote control devices to mute the commercials, putting even more of an onus on your visuals. Or they tape their TV fare, then fast-forward through the commercials. If your name and prime benefit are not communicated visually, you are wasting money.

Properly used, TV can be fascinating, fun to watch, motivating, informative to your prospects, and profitable for you. As you can probably surmise, TV is not a do-it-yourself venture. It is also not something you can turn over to the TV station.

Perhaps they should produce it for you, but let a sales-minded pro write it for you—creating a script that contains the words and a description of the visuals. Done right—meaning centered around an idea rather than a special effect—TV can be guerrilla dynamite! Guerrillas who do it right love it. I have a strong feeling that you can learn to love it, too. Just be sure you realize that your role in television is not entertainment, but marketing.

Outdoor Billboards

In most cases, outdoor billboards work best if they tie in with your marketing campaign conducted in other media, such as newspapers, TV, radio, or magazines.

When any or all of these mass media are utilized, a billboard campaign, generally consisting of multiple billboard locations, can serve as an excellent reminder medium—if your basic message is succinct enough.

In billboard parlance, this means six words. Can you make your marketing point using a visual device and just six words? Marlboro has successfully used billboards with only one word, and sometimes two (when they used "Marlboro Country"). But they had millions more to invest in billboards than most guerrillas. That, plus a guerrilla's imagination and commitment.

Billboards are also extremely valuable if you can honestly write these magic words on them: NEXT EXIT; ranking on up there for creativity are TWO MILES AHEAD and 5 MINUTES. These are the kinds of words that generate powerful impulse reactions and result in instant sales, a rare gratification for guerrillas, who comprehend the need for patience.

When your prime market is motorists, billboards make sense. They also make sense if you are located on the same road as the billboard. Billboards are a good idea if they are the most expedient way of reaching your target market.

Billboards may be used in unusual ways, such as removing the entire inside of the billboard, and attaching a sign to the remaining frame reading: SCENERY COURTESY OF GUERRILLA MARKETING INTERNATIONAL. Some billboards have built-in light shows. Others employ an increasing array of special effects.

As in all other forms of marketing, repetition is one of the benefits you get when you rent billboard space—obtaining it for periods of a month to a year, and generally having to accept a few marginal locations along with a few choice spots.

If you supply the artwork, the billboard company will handle the production of your art onto what are generally twenty-four poster-sized sheets of paper, comprising what is termed a "twenty-four-sheet board" in the board game, if you'll excuse the pun.

A sudden showing of billboards captures attention. So does the use of billboards as part of a teaser campaign or as part of the launch of a brand-new marketing effort. But if you expect billboards to do your entire selling job, I hope you own a restaurant two miles down the road, right at the next exit, less than five minutes away.

10

A STRATEGY FOR USING THE WEAPONS

The proverbial kid in the candy store has nothing on you. You're able to use a whole new world of marketing weapons. You're swimming in marketing opportunities. You now see how you can be in control of a process that once was in control of you.

At the same time, you may be a bit overwhelmed. If you've been mentally marking the weapons you ought to be using, your head is brimming with marketing possibilities. What to do with so many?

The first thing is to get a large piece of paper and something to mark it with—a pen, typewriter, or word processor.

Second, realize that you need not activate at once all the weapons that intrigue you. Act quickly to get the process started and create your marketing momentum. This starts with a weapon described in Chapter 2, your marketing plan. When it is written, all your marketing efforts that follow can be handled with acumen since everything else will seem to fall in place. Understand that you don't have to rush. Some of my clients have taken up to eighteen months to begin firing all of the weapons in their arsenals.

Armed with your paper, writing implement, and the realization that you're not in any hurry, you're ready to get down to the nitty-gritty.

Write that marketing plan now—keeping it to seven sentences, but leaving blank—for the moment—the fourth sentence, the one that tells which marketing weapons you'll use. You'll add that sentence later.

Before you begin filling your large sheet of paper with large promises you'll be making to yourself, I want to point out the 50 guerrilla marketing weapons that are free, or at least almost free, such as follow-up and club memberships, hardly major expenses unless you join a country club with a $100,000 initiation fee. Let's return to pages 12–13 and see what these weapons are.

The question to ask yourself when perusing this list is why should you neglect any one of these weapons?

While you might be able to make a case for some of these costing money, I can make an equally strong suggestion for how to utilize them without spending any money. Remember, guerrilla marketing bestows generously and asks only time, energy, and imagination—in this case, especially imagination.

What you must do now to execute your marketing plan, activate your marketing weapons, and achieve your marketing goals is to make one four-part list, your Weapons List. It's a crucial list, and after you've put it down for the first time, you'll probably want to rewrite or retype the final version.

Although tens and perhaps hundreds of thousands of people will read this book, no two of them will create the identical list. Each, acting in true guerrilla fashion, will create a list custom-tailored to his or her specific business, budget, energy level, creative spirit, and competitive situation.

The only lists that will generate highly satisfying profits

are the lists that are actually made—rather than those that are pondered but not acted on.

Guerrillas are people of *action*. They do not theorize as much as they act. They realize that everything is difficult before it becomes simple. And they know in their guerrilla souls that there is no way to do anything with excellence if they don't do it at all.

This special breed of business owners wants to do its marketing with excellence. Since the owners have invested a few hours in reading this book, they'll gladly invest a few minutes more—perhaps a full hour more—in making the four-part Weapons List recommended by the book.

The First Part of Your Weapons List: The Weapons

Your all-important four-part Weapons List begins with a list of the weapons you wish you use. Simply go through the Contents pages and write on your sheet of paper, about one inch from the left side of the paper, each weapon you feel can benefit your business. Write clearly and don't write large.

I expect you to enlist the aid of many weapons. Keep in mind that the more weapons you use properly, the more profits you'll amass. I've been clear on that point, haven't I? Be realistic, but be optimistic as well. If ever there's a time and place to show your competitive spunk, this is it.

The Second Part of Your Weapons List: The Priorities

Now that you've got a bountiful list of weapons, decide which you wish to activate first, second, third, and so on down the line until all weapons have been activated. They sure won't all be activated at the same time, and some obviously are better suited for instant action rather than deployment down the road. So number the weapons on your list in the order you wish to use them. Write your numbers on the far left. The reason I'm being so primer-clear on this is because I'm so devoted to making a serious increase in your profits.

If one weapon is up at number two and another is down at number fifty-two, don't worry. All of them will be detonated in due time. Right now you're establishing the most effective firing order. As you must be aggressive in compiling your list, you must be judicious in prioritizing it. Program your efforts for successful launching.

The Third Part of Your Weapons List: The People

Next to each weapon, write the name of the person who will provide the primary energy in launching and maintaining the weapon. Although the ultimate responsibility may rest with you or with your designated guerrilla, most likely the grunt work will be done by a professional, an assistant, or an outside source. Write down exactly who will do what. Each weapon requires both a priority order and the name of a person who will ride herd over it.

The strategic thinking for each weapon will be guided by your overall marketing strategy, easing that burden. But the actual writing, drawing, photographing, printing, training, and other tasks will be assigned to others. The weakest links in your marketing chain will be those that are missing and those that are assigned to weaklings.

The Fourth Part of Your Weapons List: The Timing

Now that you've decided what weapons to use, the best order in which to use them, and the people who will be at the trigger, all that remains is for you to figure exactly when to activate the weapons. It's perfectly legal to write down a weapon and decide to use it in three years. What counts here is that you are making a promise to yourself with each date you put down.

So write the month and year that you will activate each of your weapons. When you have completed this, you will have a lethal document—a full-fledged guerrilla Weapons List, telling the weapons, the order of usage, the person in charge, and the time you'll fire the weapon.

It's a heady feeling, holding this document in your hands. Suddenly, you realize that the mystique has been removed from marketing. Instead of marketing being some vague and expensive process that controls you, it becomes apparent that you have full control over marketing—and that it is a key to attaining your loftiest goals.

In fact, once you begin to activate your Weapons List, there's a very good chance that you'll redefine and raise your goals. This is not an infrequent occurrence when ordinary businesspeople become transformed into marketing guerrillas.

A word about the best of these guerrillas: They place balance and freedom ahead of growth and greed. They recognize the role that work plays in their lives and they never make their work all they have in their lives. Guerrillas have the wisdom to be attracted to success and to be repelled by workaholism. They are even more careful about their time than they are about their marketing.

So they do what they can to put their marketing weapons

onto "automatic pilot"—delegating the tasks to firms and people who will perform them energetically, yet flawlessly. Even when selecting their weaponry, they keep a keen eye for the appropriateness of the weapon to their business, their budget, their manpower, their ability to deal with success, and their dreams.

Perhaps you want an impressive full-color brochure with a flap in the inside of the rear cover to hold specific documents, illustrations, and price lists. But it is not currently feasible to create, produce, and disseminate such a brochure. Not to worry. The timing will be right later.

Don't forget that marketing is judged by quality, value, and speed. Most business owners utilize any two. Guerrillas, blessed with patience, get all three. They use weapons when it is comfortable for them, not when it is expected of them.

All this guerrilla marketing is not left to chance or intuition. It is spelled out in black and white by a marketing plan and a Weapons List. Eventually, guerrillas engage in massive amounts of marketing on many fronts, outmarketing the competitors at every turn, yet underspending them.

And they continue to become more and more skilled in their marketing. As Oliver Wendell Holmes said, "Man's mind, once stretched by a new idea, never regains its original dimensions." Even Abraham Lincoln displayed his guerrilla bent when he reminded us, "Things may come to those who wait, but only the things left by those who hustle."

It's going to take a fair amount of hustling to use all the guerrilla marketing weapons you want to use, but it's also going to be fun. Winning is always fun.

CONTINUE BEING A GUERRILLA WITH THE GUERRILLA MARKETING NEWSLETTER

THE GUERRILLA MARKETING NEWSLETTER provides you with state-of-the-moment insights to maximize the profits you will obtain through marketing. The newsletter has been created to furnish you with the cream of the new guerrilla marketing information from around the world. It is filled with practical advice, the latest research, upcoming trends, and brand-new marketing techniques—all designed to pay off on your bottom line.

All issues of THE GUERRILLA MARKETING NEWSLETTER are rich with data that can help your company. Just one issue can pay for a year's subscription—even ten years' subscription. Still, if you aren't convinced after examining your first issue for 30 days that THE GUERRILLA MARKETING NEWSLETTER will raise your profits, your subscription fee will be refunded along with $2 just for trying.

THE GUERRILLA MARKETING NEWSLETTER, written by Jay Conrad Levinson, is available only by subscription. The rate is $49 per year—which includes six issues. To subscribe or to obtain information on guerrilla marketing products, videotapes, audiotapes, workshops, lectures, and services for your company, call toll-free 1-800-748-6444. In California, call 415-381-8361. That is also the Guerrilla Marketing fax number. Or write, Guerrilla Marketing International, 260 Cascade Drive, P.O. Box 1336, Mill Valley, CA 94942, U.S.A.